# 1984

*George Orwell*

AUTHORED by Christina Shelby
UPDATED AND REVISED by Jordan Berkow

COVER DESIGN by Table XI Partners LLC
COVER PHOTO by Olivia Verma and © 2005 GradeSaver, LLC

BOOK DESIGN by Table XI Partners LLC



Published by GradeSaver LLC, www.gradesaver.com

First published in the United States of America by GradeSaver LLC. 2007



ISBN 978-1-60259-114-1

Printed in the United States of America

For other products and additional information please visit
http://www.gradesaver.com

# Table of Contents

# Table of Contents

# Biography of George Orwell (1903-1950)

George Orwell was born Eric Arthur Blair on June 25, 1903, in Motihari, India. The Blairs were relatively prosperous civil servants, working in India on behalf of the British Empire. Blair would later describe his family's socioeconomic status as "lower-upper middle class," a categorization commenting on the extraordinary degree to which British citizens in India depended on the Empire for their livelihood. Though the Blairs were able to live quite comfortably in India, they had none of the physical assets or independent investments that would have been enjoyed by their class in England proper. Ida Blair moved back to England in 1904 with Eric and his older sister Marjorie so that the children could be brought up in a more traditional, Christian environment.

In England, Blair entered the public school system, and was admitted to Eton College in 1917. For most students of this era, Eton led directly to higher education at a university, often Oxford or Cambridge. Blair, however, shunned further formal schooling, and after leaving Eton in 1921 returned to India in 1922 to join the Indian Imperial Police. This work gave Blair his first real experiences with the poor and downtrodden whom he would later champion. Unhappy with being perceived as the "hand of the oppressor" in his police position, Blair resigned from the force in 1927 and returned to England that same year.

In England, Blair lived in the East End district of London. At the time, the area was filled with the destitute, whom he saw as the spiritual kin of the Burmese peasants he had encountered as a policeman. In 1928, Blair moved to Paris to become a writer. There, he again lived among the poor, and even temporarily worked as a dishwasher. He returned to England the next year (1929), and found work as a private school teacher. In this position, Blair found time to write, and his first book, *Down and Out in Paris and London*, was published in 1933 under the pseudonym George Orwell (the name by which he shall hereafter be referred to). The publication of this first work, which is an account of his years living among the poor of Paris and London, marks the beginning of a more stable period for Orwell, in which he taught, opened a bookshop, and continued to write. His first fictional work, *Burmese Days*, was published in 1934.

The next few years saw a steady stream of activity for Orwell, who produced *A Clergyman's Daughter* in 1935 and *Keep the Aspidistra Flying* in 1936. During this period he also met Eileen Maud O'Shaughnessy, whom he married on June 9, 1936. That same year Orwell received a grant from the Left Book Club to produce a work dealing with the conditions of the poor, which resulted in the publication of *The Road to Wigan Pier*. In December 1936, during the Spanish Civil War, Orwell decided to enlist in the POAM, the Socialist military party in Spain. Attracted by the vision of a society without class distinction, Orwell fought for socialism in Spain, but after being wounded in the neck was forced to return to England in 1938. He published an account of his experiences in Spain in *Homage to Catalonia* that same year.

In 1941, Orwell went to work for the BBC as a broadcaster for India, a post which he resigned to become the literary editor for the *Tribune*. This position was equally short-lived, however, as Orwell resigned in 1945 to begin work on Animal Farm. Orwell's family life experienced significant upheaval during this period, marked by the adoption of a son, Richard, in 1944, and his wife's death during an operation in 1945. Soon after Eileen's death, Animal Farm was published, and Orwell immediately became famous. In response to his sudden celebrity status, Orwell moved to the island of Jura, off the coast of Scotland, which aggravated the tuberculosis he had acquired upon returning from Spain. While at Jura, Orwell wrote his last and perhaps most famous novel, *1984*, and married Sonia Bromwell. In 1949 Orwell returned to England, suffering from painfully advanced tuberculosis. On January 21, 1950, he finally succumbed to the disease.

# About 1984

In *1984*, George Orwell presents his vision of dystopia, a world consisting of three massive totalitarian states constantly at war with each other and using technological advancements to keep their respective Party members and masses under careful observation and control. Written in 1948 and published in 1949, this novel is often touted as one of the greatest novels written in the English language.

In writing the work, Orwell was influenced and inspired by totalitarian regimes of the time, including Hitler's Nazi Germany and Stalin's Soviet Union. Both regimes glorified their respective leaders as demi-gods and saviors, required the destruction of all individuality in order to promote the Party's needs over the individual's, demanded absolute loyalty from their citizens, and resorted to violence whenever disloyalty was suspected. Moreover, both regimes consistently demonized their enemies, just as the Party and Big Brother do in *1984*, through the Two Minutes Hate, Hate Week, and daily mass propaganda. Other parallels include the Thought Police as a reinvention of the Gestapo, NKVD (People's Comissariat for Internal Affairs), which orchestrated large scale purges and terror, and the Spies and Youth League as a reinvention of the Hitler Youth and the Little Octoberists, which indoctrinated young people to the Party and encouraged them to report disloyalty observed in their elders, even among family members.

The similarities between *1984*'s Oceania and Stalin's regime are particularly striking. Like Stalin, the Oceanian government embraces characteristics of both fascist and communist authoritarianism: the former glorifies the wisdom of the leader, and the latter, the infallibility of the Party. We can see both trends in *1984*, where Big Brother (albeit apparently a fictitious entity) is worshipped as a wise and loving leader, and the Party is practically structured around its own supposed infallibility. In addition, many of the particulars of the Oceanian system, such as the Three-Year Plans and the forced labor camps, appear to be thinly veiled allusions to aspects of Stalin's rule. It is even often suggested that Oceania's Big Brother, with his dark hair and heavy mustache, is inspired by the larger-than-life images of Josef Stalin's visage so commonly seen in the Soviet Union.

Orwell's time working with the Indian Imperial Police in Burma introduced him to the shameful activities of the British in the Far East, and appears to have encouraged his exploration of the lives of the urban poor. After returning to Europe, Orwell continued to focus on this subject and began to develop a vague distrust of machine-age capitalist society that later blossomed into a firm adherence to Socialism, bolstered by his time working with the revolutionary Marxist POUM (Partido Obrero de Unificacion Marxista, or Worker's Party of Marxist Unification), the dissident faction of the Spanish Communist party. However, when the Stalin-backed Communists turned on their far-left anarchist allies and labeled POUM pro-fascist, Orwell fled to avoid prison, or worse, death. This experience taught Orwell the danger of abandoning true Socialist revolutionary ideals, and he developed both a fixation on totalitarianism and an abhorrence for Stalinist Communism, both of which are clearly expressed in *1984*. World War II's introduction of totalitarianism through fascist and communist regimes solidified Orwell's hatred of the ideology.

During the war, Orwell was equally unimpressed by his experience in Britain. From 1940-1943, Orwell was employed by the BBC, under the control of the British Ministry of Information, which served as inspiration for Winston's position at the Ministry of Truth, and perhaps for Newspeak. In this capacity, Orwell witnessed the propagation of stories glorifying Britain's triumphs while the British Empire was simultaneously steadily declining. This type of disconnect between reality and the information disseminated to the public clearly makes its way into the novel.

It is unclear to what extent Orwell believed *1984* to be an accurate prediction of the future, but many critics agree that he wrote the book as a warning to modern society of the damage that can come from embracing totalitarian regimes. The novel mourns the loss of personal identity while demonstrating how to effectively rid a person of their independence, particularly through extensive sexual repression and the prohibition of individual thought. Many of the concepts and themes presented in *1984* have steadily made their way into the common vernacular. For instance, the phrase "Big Brother" is often used to refer to the advancement and expansion of technology used to observe and record behavior, such as video cameras placed on city streets and government monitoring of phone and Internet communication. The adjective "Orwellian" is also commonly used to describe such real-world developments reminiscent of *1984*.

Orwell wrote *1984* while seriously ill with tuberculosis, and afterward commented that had he not been so ill, the book might not have been so bleak. To his consternation, after its publication, *1984* was used as propaganda itself, especially by Western forces in post-World War II Germany. Much later, there were many attempts to censor the novel, particularly on the grounds that it contains pro-Communist material and sexual references. The book has also been adapted to both television shows and movies, and has served as inspiration for a variety of other artistic endeavors, such as David Bowie's Diamond Dogs album, which includes a song titled *1984*.

# Character List

### Winston Smith

The novel's protagonist. Winston is a quiet 39-year-old man living in Oceania in the year 1984. A Party member, Winston works at the Ministry of Truth correcting "errors" in past publications. Winston is also an amateur intellectual who nurses a secret hatred of the Party. To protect himself from discovery, Winston goes through the motions of outward orthodoxy, but relishes his internal world of dreams, memories and speculation about the past. Winston is married but separated, and has no children. Upon meeting Julia, he finds an outlet for his heretical opinions and for the love he yearns to share with another human being. His physical and mental health improves, and Winston starts to believe more powerfully in an established covert movement against the Party. Unfortunately, the affair is short-lived, and the couple is arrested. Winston is taken to the Ministry of Love and subjected to extensive torture and humiliation, which force him into submission. As a result of this experience, Winston loses all rebellious thoughts, gains unadulterated love for Big Brother and the Party, and eradicates his love for Julia. In short, Winston loses his humanity. Upon his release, he is a shell of a man, yet also an ideal, loyal, and devoted Party member.

### Julia

A 26-year-old Party member who works in the Fiction Department of the Ministry of Truth. Julia also secretly despises the Party, but accepts its rule over her and therefore outwardly appears to be zealously devoted to the Party's causes. Julia declares her love for Winston, thus beginning their affair and setting them down the path towards their eventual imprisonment. Unlike Winston, Julia sees life simply, and is interested only in her survival and personal rebellion against the Party - not in long-term plans for the resurgence of democracy. Julia is arrested along with Winston and tortured in the Ministry of Love. When they meet again after their respective releases, Julia is spiritless, physically broken, and even nurses a vague dislike for Winston. Just like Winston, Julia leaves the Ministry of Love as a mere shell of a human being.

### O'Brien

A prominent Inner Party member with whom Winston feels a strange bond. Winston feels that even if O'Brien is an enemy, it wouldn't matter because he knows O'Brien will understand him without explanation. O'Brien is a large, graceful, and clearly intelligent man who leads Winston to believe he is part of an underground movement against the Party, but in fact helps turn Winston in for thoughtcrime and tortures him in the Ministry of Love. O'Brien is full of strange contradictions. He can be fatherly - and even tender - even while fanatically expressing his devotion to the Party by torturing Winston.

### Big Brother

The symbol of Oceania and the Party, Big Brother is Oceania's supreme leader, and is omnipresent through telescreen projections, coins, and even large posters warning, "BIG BROTHER IS WATCHING YOU." Big Brother is theoretically one of the original founders of the Party and the Revolution, but Winston assumes he does not exist, will never age, and will never die. He is the mouthpiece of the Party, and the symbol all Party members worship.

**Mrs. Parsons**

The wife of Tom Parsons and neighbor of Winston's. A tired, aged woman with "dust in the creases of her face," Mrs. Parsons is the mother of two horrific children belonging to the Spies and Youth League and who are bound to eventually denounce her and her husband to the Thought Police. At the beginning of the novel, Mrs. Parsons knocks on Winston's door when he is writing in his diary to ask for his help unclogging the kitchen sink. Winston obliges.

**Tom Parsons**

Husband to Mrs. Parsons, and Winston's neighbor and coworker. Tom is a heavy, sweaty, simple man whom Winston despises for his unquestioning acceptance of everything the Party tells him. Parsons is active in his community groups, and appears to truly believe Party claims and doctrine. However, his daughter eventually denounces him to the Thought Police, claiming he was saying "Down with Big Brother" in his sleep. Winston sees Tom while imprisoned in the Ministry of Love, and Tom is ironically proud of his seven-year-old daughter for having done her duty.

**Tillotson**

A coworker of Winston's, Tillotson sits across from him in the Records Department and is extremely secretive about his work.

**Ampleforth**

A coworker of Winston's, and a poet who works in the Records Department rewriting politically or ideologically objectionable Oldspeak poems. By the end of the novel, Ampleforth is in prison along with Winston, for, he believes having left the word "God" in one of his poems.

**Syme**

A "friend" of Winston's and a philologist working on the Eleventh Edition of the Newspeak Dictionary. Although Winston dislikes Syme, he enjoys having somewhat interesting conversations with him. Winston notices that Syme, although a devoted Party member, is too smart and too vocal for his own good. He predicts Syme will be vaporized, and is proven correct when he suddenly disappears.

### Katharine

Winston's wife, who never appears directly in the book but is discussed at some length. Winston describes her as "unthinkful" and claims she was absurdly devoted to the Party, to the point where she referred to sleeping with Winston to produce offspring as her "duty to the Party." The two never had children, and eventually separated. In a conversation with Julia, Winston reveals he was once tempted to murder Katharine when they were separated from others on a nature walk. However, he did not, and he assumes Katharine still lives, although he has not seen her in years.

### Mr. Charrington

The owner of the antique shop where Winston first buys his diary, pen, and later on a glass paperweight. Winston rents the room above the shop from Mr. Charrington for his love affair with Julia. Mr. Charrington appears to be a kind old man interested in history and the past, but later reveals himself to be a member of the Thought Police. Mr. Charrington leads Winston and Julia into his trap, and observes their action from the hidden telescreen in the room above the shop. As he is being arrested, Winston notices that Mr. Charrington looks entirely different, and has clearly been working under disguise for quite some time.

### Martin

O'Brien's servant, Martin is a small, dark-haired man who Winston believes might be Chinese. He leads Winston and Julia into O'Brien's apartment and sits in on their meeting, but does not speak.

### Comrade Withers

A former prominent Inner Party member who received the Order of Conspicuous Merit, Second Class. The subject of a "correction" Winston must make at the Ministry of Truth after Withers is vaporized.

### Comrade Ogilvy

A man Winston invents to replace Comrade Withers when "correcting" the news story surrounding the honors Withers, an unperson, received from the Party.

### Jones, Aaronson and Rutherford

Three Inner Party members wrongly arrested in 1965 and forced to incriminate themselves of various crimes, including treason and murder. They are eventually killed. Winston finds a clipping proving their innocence and destroys the document, but never forgets holding the proof that Party "fact" was fiction.

### Wilsher

A coworker of Winston's who delays his first conversation with Julia by inviting Winston to sit with him in the canteen.

**Prole Washer Woman**

A large, brawny, stocky prole woman who is constantly hanging laundry and singing below the window in Mr. Charrington's apartment.

**Starving Man**

A man briefly placed in Winston's holding cell who is clearly being starved to death. When told to go to Room 101 he tells them to take the man who offered him food (Bumstead) instead - anything but 101.

**Bumstead**

A prisoner in the Ministry of Love who offers the starving man a piece of old bread. He is immediately punished with a violent attack that breaks his jaw and causes heavy bleeding.

# Major Themes

### Totalitarianism

In writing *1984*, Orwell's main goal was to warn of the serious danger totalitarianism poses to society. He goes to great lengths to demonstrate the terrifying degree of power and control a totalitarian regime can acquire and maintain. In such regimes, notions of personal rights and freedoms and individual thought are pulverized under the all-powerful hand of the government. Orwell was a Socialist and believed strongly in the potential for rebellion to advance society, yet too often he witnessed such rebellions go wrong and develop into totalitarian rule. Specifically, Orwell saw such developments during his time in Spain and in Russia, where he witnessed the rise of communism and the accompanying destruction of civil liberties, honest government, and economic strength.

During a time when much of the Western world was lauding communism as a step towards human progress in the development of equality in government, Orwell clearly and definitively spoke out against the practice. In *1984*, Orwell presents a dystopia, or in other words, the perfect totalitarian state. In composing this novel, Orwell gave the world a glimpse of what the embrace of communism might lead to if allowed to proceed unchecked. The Party is unflawed in its universal control over society, as evidenced by its ability to break even an independent thinker such as Winston, and has mastered every aspect of psychological control, largely through utilizing technological developments (allowing for inventions such as the telescreen) to their advantage. In ending the novel with Winston defeated in every sense of the term, Orwell clearly suggests that there is no hope for quelling the expansion or growth of such a perfectly established regime. And, more importantly, Orwell warns that at the time, this outcome was within the realm of possibility as long as the world supported and embraced communism.

### Propaganda

A major factor in the Party's rule over Oceania lies in its extremely well organized and effective propaganda machine. The Ministry of Truth, which is ironically where Winston works, is responsible for disseminating all Party publications and information. All figures and facts come from the Ministry of Truth, and all are dictated by the Party. In other words, the Party chooses exactly what to tell the public, regardless of what is accurate. The effectiveness of this propaganda machine, which constantly corrects old material to reflect the Party's current position on any subject ranging from chocolate rations to the loyalty of a specific individual, allows the Party to completely dominate the range of information disseminated to the public. Therefore, as O'Brien notes, the machine determines what constitutes reality.

In addition to the massive amounts of doctored information the Party disseminates to the public, there are also basic forms of propaganda, such as the Two Minutes

Hate, Hate Week, posters of Big Brother, and required daily participation in the Physical Jerks. The Party uses literally every waking opportunity to instill its ideals into its citizens, and is strikingly successful in achieving its goal of total loyalty. In *1984* we see the vigor and loyalty such propaganda inspires in the citizens. The citizens of Oceania are filled with hatred for the country's stated enemies, but this hatred is easily re-directed if the enemy happens to change. This efficiency is quite disturbing. Orwell's presentation of the power of propaganda significantly supports his warning against totalitarianism. If propaganda rules all information, it is impossible to have any grasp on reality. The world is as the Party defines it.

### Love/Sexuality

The Party works to quell all physical sensations of love, and depersonalizes sex to the point where it is referred to as a "duty to the Party" (for the purposes of procreation). Some Party organizations even advocate complete abstinence and procreation only through artificial insemination. Winston suffers the Party's removal of personal fulfillment or enjoyment in relationships in his failed marriage with Katharine. Later, when he finds Julia, Winston relishes the freedom of being able to love someone in a physical and emotional way. So much of Winston's seeming rebellion turns out to be guided and influenced by the Party (Mr. Charrington, O'Brien, the Brotherhood), but his relationship with Julia is not. Winston is only able to rebel against the Party through his affair with Julia, even though this love is destroyed in the end.

Orwell's discussion of love is not only relegated to romantic love. Through Winston's memories of his mother and the contrast between how she cared for him and his sister and the average Party family is striking. Winston's mother deeply loved her children and did all she could to protect them during the aftermath of the Revolution and the Party's rise to power. In Winston's time, the Party has removed such interfamilial loyalty, demanding that all love and loyalty be reserved for Big Brother and the Party. In this way, the bonds between parents and children are broken. Even worse, children commonly report their parents to the Thought Police, placing the Party above the lives of their mother and father. The Party's eventual goal is to destroy the family unit entirely and have all children raised in Party facilities. The Party has no room for love, unless that love is directed with full force at Big Brother and Oceania.

### Independence/Identity

Through its effective psychological manipulation tactics, the Party destroys all sense of independence and individuality. Everyone wears the same clothes, eats the same food, and lives in the same grungy apartments. Life is uniform and orderly. No one can stand out, and no one can be unique. To have an independent thought borders on the criminal. For this reason, writing such as Winston does in his diary has been outlawed. People are only permitted to think what the Party tells them to think, which leads to what Syme refers to as "duckspeak." Independent thought can be dangerous, as it might lead to rebellion.

This theme comes to a head during Winston's torture, when Winston argues that he is a man, and because he is a man O'Brien cannot tell him what he thinks. O'Brien counters that if Winston is a man, he is the last man on earth. Moreover, O'Brien suggests that this independence is evidence of insanity. O'Brien's view represents the purity of a totalitarian regime, in that independent thought must be destroyed to promote the needs and goals of the Party. Winston and Julia's downfall occurs because they believe they are special. Their arrest and torture, however, breaks this spirit. Once again, through this ultimate loss of individual thought, we witness Orwell's warning against embracing any version of totalitarian rule.

**Music**

Songs appear throughout the novel, most often when Winston is reflecting on the state of the world. Music appears to inspire Winston and allows him to see beauty and simplicity in an otherwise violent, ugly, and frightening world. He sees a powerful sense of tragedy in "Under the spreading Chestnut Tree," hope for a brighter future in the beautiful thrush song, respect for the true, untouchable past in the "St. Clement's Dane" rhyme, and freedom and hope in the passion with which the prole woman sings while hanging her laundry. Below, listed in chronological order are the musical events that occur in the novel.

Winston describes sitting in the Chestnut Tree Cafe, observing the clearly beaten, defeated, and tragically sad Jones, Aaronson and Rutherford, while the song "Under the spreading Chestnut Tree, I sold you and you sold me" plays over the telescreen. The song seems to reflect the broken spirits of these three men, who were once Inner Party members and now have lost everything.

Mr. Charrington teaches Winston the rhyme that begins "Oranges and lemons say the bells of St. Clement's," which is a vestige of the past. Throughout the novel, Winston holds on to this rhyme and tries to discover its entirety. He succeeds, with the help of Julia, who remembers a few more lines than Mr. Charrington, and O'Brien, who finishes the poem for Winston.

Julia and Winston are in the Golden Country, beginning their affair. As they stand next to each other surveying the landscape, a small thrush begins to sing next to them. Winston is taken in by the bird's boundless freedom and wonders what makes him sing so beautifully. To Winston, the bird's song represents all he longs for in life. It is the exact opposite of the Party.

Winston hears the prole woman in the yard behind Mr. Charrington's house sing while she works. She belts out the tune without any hesitation, throwing herself into the simple music with a passion Winston reveres.

Winston tells Julia of the poem Mr. Charrington taught him, and she adds two verses. Her grandfather taught her the rhyme when she was young, and Winston is elated to learn the next few lines of the piece. This cooperation reveals a strong bond between Winston and Julia.

Winston discusses the Hate Song the Party created solely for the Hate Week celebration. This is the only time we hear of a song created purely for negative means. Winston notes that the Hate Song is not as popular among the proles as some of the more simple tunes the Ministry of Truth has produced for them.

O'Brien completes Mr. Charrington's rhyme, and Winston is immensely satisfied to finally know the complete piece. He feels that gaining the last puzzle piece from O'Brien symbolically represents their bond in rebelling against the Party and pursuing a future steeped in freedom.

Winston again hears the prole woman singing passionately while doing her wash and reflects on the primitivism in song. Winston thinks about the millions of people around the world, just like this woman, who find such pleasure, power and freedom in music and are able to embrace it in their lives. He is arrested immediately after this brief scene, which fulfills the last line of the "St. Clement's Dane" song, "Here comes a chopper to chop off your head!"

Winston sits in the Chestnut Tree Cafe, just as Jones, Aaronson and Rutherford once did. He hears the same song he heard when watching those three men, "Under the spreading Chestnut Tree, I sold you and you sold me." Here, the song speaks to the destruction of Winston's independence, and his newly discovered love for Big Brother.

### Loyalty

The Party is fueled by loyalty, and thus demands that its citizens support any and all actions it takes in pursuing a greater Oceania. For the Party, loyalty means accepting without question or hesitation. Ironically, when Winston pledges his loyalty to the Brotherhood, he also agrees to accept the goals and requirements of the Brotherhood without question or hesitation. Winston agrees to do anything the Brotherhood requires, even if that means murdering innocents. However, Winston is also loyal to Julia, and refuses to be separated from her forever. This split loyalty is what separates Winston from the other Party members. Party members are loyal to the Party, Big Brother, and Oceania alone. Personal relationships are of no importance.

While in the Ministry of Love, O'Brien notes this weakness in Winston's mind and effectively removes it. Through painful physical torture, O'Brien first teaches Winston that the Party's perspective is the accurate perspective. Next, by threatening him with carnivorous rats, O'Brien breaks Winston's loyalty to Julia. In the last scene of the novel, Winston finally comes to love Big Brother, and his transition from split loyalties to a greater single loyalty to the Party is complete.

## Poverty vs. Wealth

Oceanian society presents a clear dichotomy in living conditions. The small Inner Party lives luxuriously, with servants and lush, well-furnished apartments. Party members, on the other hand, live in run-down single-room apartments with no amenities and low-quality, tasteless food. The proles live in absolute poverty. The chasm between poverty and wealth in the novel is striking, and is most noticeable during Winston's forays into prole society. The buildings the proles live in are decaying, and the city of London is filled with bombed-out ruins. While the Inner Party comforts itself with luxury, the citizens of Oceania suffer, getting by with the bare minimum in a dying city.

Orwell presents this dichotomy to demonstrate how totalitarian societies promote the wealth of the ruling regime while decreasing the quality of life for all other members of society. Such governments often tout their hopes for establishing an equal society when in reality the separation between their living conditions and those of the citizens is vast. Winston looks out on the city of London and sees a dying world. Meanwhile, O'Brien looks out on the city of London and sees a society trapped in a single moment in time, defined and controlled by the Party.

## Technology

As previously noted, technology is an extremely important tool that the Party uses to maintain control over its citizens. Without telescreens, the Thought Police would not be nearly as effective, and propaganda would not be so widespread. The constant supervision of the telescreen effectively imprisons citizens of Oceania in their daily lives: they are always under observation.

Ironically, other areas of technological development are strikingly stagnant. For example, the printing machines in the Ministry of Truth are still quite basic, and each superstate continues to build the same bombs that were used decades before. Scientific progress has halted, except where it serves the Party's goals (such as in artificial insemination or new methods for psychological manipulation). In the world of Oceania there is no such as thing as progress for the sake of progress; there is only power for the sake of power. When technological developments serve this power, they are encouraged. When they do not, they are stopped.

## Language

Newspeak plays an extremely important role in Oceanian society and in the Party's control over its population. As Syme says, Newspeak reduces and limits the number of words in the English language, and removes words used to describe rebellion or independence (with the ultimate goal being to remove citizens' ability to think anti-Party thoughts). Interestingly, the Party works to form a language around itself rather than naturally accepting and assuming the language of the people that make up the country. In this way, language is used as yet another mechanism of mind control.

Removing a nation's original language serves to reduce the importance of a nation's past. Languages develop over centuries, and are deeply intertwined with culture and history. Redefining and forcing a language on a population, as was often done in the postcolonial era, denies that society its individuality. The Party meets this goal with great efficiency.

# Glossary of Terms

**"The book"**

Titled "Theory and Practice of Oligarchical Collectivism" and supposedly written by Goldstein, it contains the story of humankind and the Revolution, arguing that there is hope for a stronger future without the dishonesty and manipulation of the Party.

**Airstrip One**

Part of Oceania, once known as Britain.

**Artsem**

Newspeak for artificial insemination.

**Black Market**

Illegal trade resource for all "good quality" materials, such as real coffee, sugar, razors, etc.

**Doublethink**

Newspeak word with two mutually contradictory meanings. The first is used to refer to an opponent, and can be defined as habitually contradicting plain facts. The second is used to refer to a Party member, and can be defined as a loyal willingness to believe contradictory statements when the Party demands it, which allows for continual alteration of the past.

**Floating Fortress**

Part of Oceania's offensive/defensive armaments. Literally an unsinkable fortress floating on the ocean.

**Hate Week**

A week of hate mongering against enemies of war. Supported by massive rallies and organized through the Ministry of Truth, Hate Week rallies Party members around Oceania and Big Brother.

**House of the Lords**

Part of the British government in the capitalist days. Referred to by an old man Winston meets at a pub, although Winston does not understand the reference or the man's meaning.

**Ingsoc**

Newspeak for English Socialism.

**Junior Anti-Sex League**

A youth organization advocating complete celibacy for both sexes and encouraging artsem. Julia is a member and wears the organization's symbolic scarlet sash.

**Jus primae noctis**

A supposed capitalist law that allowed any capitalist the right to sleep with any woman working in one of his factories. A "fact" the party cites about capitalist history.

**Ministry of Love (Miniluv)**

Maintains law and order. Protected with great force. Only those arrested for Thought Crime or who are on official Party business can enter. Referred to within the novel as "the place with no darkness" because the lights are always on. Dissidents are taken here to be tortured, reformed, or killed.

**Ministry of Peace (Minipax)**

Responsible for the Party's management of issues surrounding war.

**Ministry of Plenty (Miniplenty)**

Responsible for the Party's economic affairs.

**Ministry of Truth (Minitrue)**

Responsible for all Party news, entertainment, education and fine arts. The Party's propaganda machine.

**Newspeak**

The official language of Oceania and the new language of the Party, devised to meet the ideological needs of Ingsoc (English Socialism). The goal of Newspeak is to reduce the English language to the fewest words possible and supercede Oldspeak by 2050. Removing words removes ways to define anti-Party feelings and the ability to disagree. For example, the word "speedful" can be used in place of the word "rapid."

**Party Slogans**

Examples include: "War is Peace"; "Freedom is Slavery"; "Ignorance is Strength."

**Pornosec**

The area of the Fiction Department in the Ministry of Truth devoted to creating written pornographic material for the proles. Dominated by women because the Party believes women are less likely to be corrupted by the material.

**Prole**

One of the 85% of the Oceania population that are not Party members and live in poverty. Regulated loosely to weed out the overly intellectual and protect the Party.

**Reclamation Centers**

Colonies for homeless children.

**Saccharine**

A chemical sweetener or sugar substitute; excessively sweet.

**Spanner**

Wrench.

**Speakwrite**

A party tool used to translate spoken word into written word.

**Spies and Youth League**

A Party youth organization that encourages children to spy on and report elders, including parents, to the Thought Police. Indoctrinates children into the Party.

**St. Clement's Dane**

A building bombed many years ago that once stood by the Law Courts in London. A rendering of the building hangs on the wall in Mr. Charrington's rented room and turns out to be a hidden telescreen.

**Telescreen**

An oblong metal plaque that looks like a dulled mirror and acts like a television, a camera, and a listening device for the Inner Party and Thought Police. There is no way to shut it off completely, and it keeps tabs on all Party members.

**The Physical Jerks**

Daily morning exercises all Party members must take part in. Dictated via the telescreen.

**The Revolution**

The rise of new socialism (versus democracy and capitalism) that resulted in Ingsoc in Oceania, Neo-Bolshevism in Eurasia, and Death Worship in Eastasia. Each regime has the conscious aim of perpetuating unfreedom and inequality, arresting progress, freezing history in a chosen moment, and perpetuating war.

**The Times**

A Party-sponsored news publication for which Winston works.

**Thought Police**

The arm of the Inner Party that seeks out those against the Party, searching out anyone with even the smallest thoughts against the Party or Big Brother. Their powers of observation force everyone to live as though they are always being watched or listened to. Mr. Charrington is a member.

**Thoughtcrime**

Thinking against the Party, having misgivings about the Party, doubting Big Brother, or questioning any Party action or "fact."

**Tube**

Subway system.

**Two Minutes Hate**

Daily requirement for all Party members. Organized group of members watches Party presentations on a telescreen denouncing Goldstein and war enemies (either Eastasia or Eurasia), and celebrating Big Brother. Causes great outbursts of hatred such as directed screaming and violence at screen representations of the enemy.

**Vaporized**

The fate of those who commit Thoughtcrimes. Those who are vaporized are removed from society in that they are killed and all evidence of their existence is removed.

**Victory products**

Party-made products, such as gin, cigarettes, clothing, food, and even housing. All of poor quality.

# Short Summary

The novel's protagonist, Winston Smith, is a citizen of Oceania, one of the world's three superstates (along with Eurasia and Eastasia). It is the year 1984, and Winston lives in Airstrip One, which used to be known as Great Britain. Winston is a member of the Party, which rules Oceania under the principles of Ingsoc (English Socialism). Oceania is an oligarchy, under hierarchical rule. The Party consists of Inner Party members, who are the ruling elite, and regular Party members, who are citizens of Oceania. Outside of the Party are the proles, non-Party members and simple people who live in poverty and are free from Party regulations. The Party's leader is Big Brother, and there are massive images of his kind visage, complete with dark hair and a substantial mustache, displayed throughout London, some accompanied by the words "Big Brother is Watching You." The Party's three slogans are: "War is Peace," "Freedom is Slavery," and "Ignorance is Strength."

Winston lost his parents and little sister during the Revolutionary period that destroyed capitalism and instituted Ingsoc in Oceania. He was placed in a Party orphanage and integrated into the Party system. Now he works in the Records Department of the Ministry of Truth, which handles all Party publications and propaganda, altering previously published Party publications to ensure that the Party's version of the Past is never questioned. Such alterations often remove a person from history, or make previously flawed predictions accurate. The other three ministries are the Ministry of Love, which handles all Party prisoners, the Ministry of Peace, which handles war, and the Ministry of Plenty, which manages the production of Party goods, including Victory cigarettes, Victory gin, and Victory coffee, all of which are of extremely poor quality.

Winston has never quite accepted the principles of Ingsoc and the Party. He believes in an unalterable past, and finds Party politics reprehensible. Winston wishes for privacy, intimacy, freedom and love, but cannot express any of this in the open for fear of death. Such thoughts constitute "throughtcrimes," which are highly punishable offenses resulting in arrest, imprisonment, torture, and often death.

When the book opens, Winston is at home during his lunch break. He has returned to his apartment in the Victory Mansions, a dilapidated Party housing building, to write in a diary, a relic of the past he obtained from an old junk shop. Winston's apartment is meager, and like every other Party member's home, contains a telescreen. The telescreen transmits Party information and propaganda, and also allows the Thought Police to watch and listen to Party members at all times. In Oceania, there is no such thing as privacy. Winston is fortunate to have a small nook in his apartment out of the view of the telescreen, and it is in this nook that he begins to write in his diary, despite his overwhelming fear of being caught. Undoubtedly, Winston will eventually be caught, imprisoned, and tortured by the Thought Police. For now, however, he chooses to forge ahead with his rebellion.

Winston writes of various memories, all related to the Party and his life. Many include violent imagery, which is quite common in the age of Oceania, and reveal anti-Party feelings. Winston clearly does not subscribe to Party doctrine. Winston is briefly interrupted at one point by a knock on his door. At first he panics, thinking he has already been caught, but it is only his neighbor, Mrs. Parsons, who needs help unclogging her sink. Winston obliges, and interacts briefly with Mrs. Parsons' two hellish children who are members of the Spies and Youth League, and clearly powerfully indoctrinated in the ways of the Party. Winston predicts that eventually these children will turn their loyal, simple, innocent parents into the Thought Police. Such tragedies, it seems, are quite common.

Winston returns to his diary, and in one of his reveries reflecting on the past and his memories and dreams, finds himself writing "DOWN WITH BIG BROTHER" in large letters over and over on the page. Eventually, time runs out and Winston must return to work, which he enjoys. Once Winston found a newspaper clipping among his daily assignments that proved the innocence of three men: Jones, Aaronson, and Rutherford. In examining the clipping, he knew it meant the Party was wrong, and that he had real evidence of an accurate version of the past. Rather than risk discovery, however, he destroyed the clipping, placing it in a memory hole that sucked it into the building's internal furnaces.

At the Ministry of Truth Winston is surrounded by loyal Party members, and is always on guard to prevent his true feelings from being perceived by others. At work, Winston sits through the daily Two Minutes Hate, which rails against Oceania's enemy, Eurasia, and the supposed leader of the opposition movement, Emmanuel Goldstein. The propaganda is powerful, and the people around him begin shouting at the screen. Of course, Winston must join in to avoid suspicion.

Finding himself increasingly curious about the past, Winston wanders the streets, among the proles. He believes that if there is hope for a successful rebellion, it lies in the proles. Winston meets an old man in a prole pub and questions him about life before the Revolution. To his frustration, the man focuses on his own personal memories rather than on the generalities and conceptual differences Winston is interested in. Winston returns to the junk shop where he bought his diary and purchases a glass paperweight with a piece of coral inside. The proprietor, a kind old man named Mr. Charrington, shows him a room above the shop and Winston thinks about what it might be like to rent it out and live among old things, free from the constant presence of the telescreen.

At work and on his walk, Winston sees a dark-haired girl who is seemingly a violently loyal Party member and apparently has taken notice of him. He fears she is a member of the Thought Police. One day, at the Ministry of Truth, the girl slips him a note after falling down in the hallway, requiring Winston's assistance. The note says "I love you." Winston is astounded, but extremely excited by the possibility of a love affair. The affair must be secret, as the Party is entirely against any sort of sexual pleasure. In fact, sexual repression is a tenet of Ingsoc. The Party must approve every marriage, and it is unacceptable for a man and a woman to express any physical attraction for one another. All energy must be devoted to the Party. Winston was once in such a marriage. His wife Katharine was a frigid, mindless woman who was extremely loyal to the Party, but thought sex was a vile activity. However, she regularly scheduled times for her and Winston to make love, calling it her "duty to the Party." She had been taught from childhood that she must bear children.

With a great deal of effort to remain undetected, the girl finally tells Winston where and how they can meet. On a Sunday afternoon, he travels into the country, as per Julia's instructions, to meet her in a secluded clearing in a wooded area. Finally, they can speak. Winston learns that her name is Julia, they discuss their beliefs regarding the Party, and they begin their love affair. At one point, Winston notices that the secluded spot she has led them to exactly matches a place he constantly sees in his dreams that he has termed the Golden Country.

Winston and Julia, who has a knack for finding abandoned locales and for obtaining black market goods such as real coffee, bread and sugar, continue to meet in secret. They are limited to interacting only in public places and having only the most minimal conversations, but the two discover a mutual hatred of the Party and eventually fall in love. Winston believes that it is possible to overthrow the Party, while Julia is satisfied simply living a double life. On the surface, she is loyal to the extreme, a member of the Junior Anti-Sex League, a volunteer in many Party activities, and a vocal participant in loyalty-testing events such as the Two Minutes Hate. On the inside, she thinks of it all as a game. She hates the Party and all it stands for, but knows she can do nothing to change it.

Eventually Winston rents the room above Mr. Charrington's flat. Winston and Julia meet often in the room, which is simply furnished, with an old twelve-hour clock (the Party uses twenty-four hour time), and a picture of an old London church, St. Clement's Dane. Mr. Charrington taught him the first lines of an old poem about the church, "Oranges and lemons say the bells of St. Clement's," and Julia knows a few more lines that her grandfather taught her when she was very small. Outside their window, a middle-aged prole woman is constantly hanging her wash and singing simple prole songs, many of which have been created by machines in the Ministry of Truth specifically for the proles.

Another Party member suddenly takes on an important role in Winston's life. Winston has always noticed O'Brien at the Ministry of Truth. He seems to be an intelligent man, and Winston believes in his heart that O'Brien feels the same way he does about the Party. Once, during the Two Minutes Hate, the two men locked eyes and Winston felt sure of O'Brien's thoughts. In a dream, Winston once heard someone tell him, "We will meet in the place where there is no darkness," and he believes the voice to have been O'Brien's. For Winston, O'Brien represents the possibility of an underground movement. Perhaps the Brotherhood, led my Emmanuel Goldstein, is real.

O'Brien approaches Winston at work under the pretense of discussing the Tenth Edition of the Newspeak Dictionary (Newspeak is the official language of Oceania, and its goal is to reduce and simplify vocabulary). O'Brien gives Winston his home address, supposedly so he can come pick up an advance copy of the new book. Winston takes the slip of paper with amazement. He knows that O'Brien has approached him because he is part of the underground movement. His true path towards rebellion has begun.

After some time, Winston and Julia visit O'Brien, an Inner Party member who has a lush apartment, a servant, and the freedom to turn off his telescreen. Winston renounces the Party and discusses his belief in the Brotherhood. O'Brien welcomes Winston and Julia into the Brotherhood and tells them that they must be willing to do anything to work towards its cause. They agree, but say that they will not do anything that would prevent them from seeing each other ever again. O'Brien tells Winston that he will give him a copy of Goldstein's book, and outlines a complicated version of events that will lead toward the exchange. Winston leaves after a final toast with O'Brien, in which Winston finishes O'Brien's statement, saying that they "will meet in the place with no darkness."

During Hate Week, the Party's enemy becomes Eastasia rather than Eurasia, and Winston must spend a great deal of time at work, sometimes even staying overnight, to "correct" all Party publications previously referring to war with Eurasia. The Party is at war with Eastasia, and *has always been* at war with Eastasia. In the midst of Hate Week, a man brings Winston a brief case, suggests that he dropped it, and leaves. The book is inside. When he has finally completed the Hate Week corrections, Winston escapes to Mr. Charrington's apartment and begins to read. Julia arrives, and he reads aloud to her about the history of Oceania, capitalism versus totalitarianism, and the main goals of the Party. Most of this information Winston already knows, but he finds it helpful to read it in the detailed, clear words of Emmanuel Goldstein.

Winston and Julia eventually fall asleep. The wake hours later, and go to stand at the window. Winston repeats his oft-stated phrase, "We are the dead." Suddenly, a voice coming from the wall echoes him, "You are the dead." There is a telescreen hidden behind the picture of St. Clement's Dane. They are caught. The Thought Police storm the room. Mr. Charrington walks in, and it becomes clear that he is a member of the Thought Police. He has been disguised as a kind old man, but is far younger than Winston imagined, with different hair and eyes. Winston and Julia are arrested, separated, and brought to the Ministry of Love.

While in a holding cell, Winston sees men from the Ministry of Truth come and go. Each has been arrested for thoughtcrime. Parsons arrives, and it turns out that his daughter turned him in, claiming to have heard him say "Down with Big Brother" in his sleep. Winston's prediction, it appears, was sadly accurate. In his holding cell, Winston sees a great deal of violence, and notices guards constantly referring to "Room 101," a phrase that seems to instill great fear in some of the prisoners.

Eventually, O'Brien arrives. It becomes clear that he was never part of the underground movement, but actually works in the Ministry of Love. Winston's entire interaction with O'Brien was a ruse. Winston is removed from the holding cell, and his torture begins. At first the torture is extremely violent, and he is forced to admit to a litany of crimes he did not commit, including murder and espionage. Eventually, the torture becomes less violent and O'Brien takes over. He begins to break Winston's spirit, telling him that his memory is flawed and that he is insane. Winston's discussions with O'Brien dwell on the nature of the past and reality, and reveal much about the Party's approach to those concepts. The Party, O'Brien explains with a lunatic intensity, seeks absolute power, for power's own sake. This is why it will always be successful, is always right, and will ultimately control the entire world. Winston cannot argue; every time he does, he is faced with obstinate logical fallacies, a completely different system of reasoning that runs counter to all reason. Winston believes in a past that never existed, and is hounded by false memories. To be cured, Winston must overcome his own insanity and win the war against his own mind.

Little by little, O'Brien shows Winston, with the use of electric shock machines, beatings and starvation, the way of the Party. He forces Winston to accept that if the Party says so, two plus two equals five. Winston had once written in his diary that freedom meant being able to say that two plus two is four. His final attempt to argue with O'Brien ends in O'Brien showing Winston himself in the mirror. Winston is beyond horrified to see that he has turned into a sickly, disgusting sack of bones, beaten into a new face. Broken to the core, Winston finally submits to his re-education. He is no longer beaten, is fed at regular intervals, is allowed to sleep (though the lights, of course, never go out), and begins to regain his health. Although seemingly making progress in accepting the reality of the Party, Winston is still holding onto the last remaining kernel of himself and his humanity: his love for Julia. This comes out when, in the midst of a dream, Winston cries aloud, "Julia! Julia! Julia, my love! Julia!"

O'Brien's last efforts with Winston are focused on forcing him to betray Julia. He takes Winston to Room 101, containing the worst thing in the world, which is different for everyone. For Winston, "the worst thing in the world" is a rat. Winston is tied to a chair, and O'Brien begins to attach a mask/cage contraption containing huge, hungry, carnivorous rats to his face. Winston feels a desperate, deep, panicked fear. He cannot take it, and finally screams for O'Brien to put someone else in his place - anyone, even Julia. O'Brien has succeeded.

Winston, a damaged, changed, empty shell of a man, is released into the world. In his new life, he sees Julia once, by chance, but they are no longer in love. Each betrayed the other, and prison changed them powerfully. There is no hope for their relationship. Winston obtains a somewhat trivial, meaningless job that pays surprisingly well. He spends his time at the Chestnut Tree Cafe drinking Victory Gin and playing chess. His life is buried in gin. In the final pages of the novel, we find Winston in his regular seat at the cafe, drinking gin, playing chess, and waiting for a report from the front in Central Africa, where Eurasia (Oceania was always at war with Eurasia) has invaded. He is excited about the report, because with this invasion, Eurasia might actually be able to break Oceania's line of defense and put the entire nation at risk for takeover. A Eurasian success in Central Africa might mean the end of the Party. Before the report comes, Winston suddenly recalls a very happy day in his childhood spent playing board games with his mother and little sister. He pushes it out of his mind, realizing it is a false memory and resolving to allow fewer of those to creep up on him. Eventually, the report reveals that Oceania has succeeded in repelling the Eurasian advance. There is jubilation on the telescreen and in the streets. Staring into the eyes of a poster of Big Brother, Winston realizes that he knew this news would come. With tears dripping down his face, Winston realizes he has finally completed the rehabilitation he started in the Ministry of Love. He loves Big Brother.

# Summary and Analysis of Part One I-II

Winston lives in the city of London, in Airstrip One. London is contained in the superstate of Oceania, formerly known as Great Britain. The opening section of the book consists largely of Winston's personal reflections on his existence and the world in which he lives. Oceania is a totalitarian state dominated by the principles of Ingsoc (English Socialism) and ruled by an ominous organization known simply as the Party, of which Big Brother is the figurehead. Two other superstates inhabit the world along with Oceania, Eurasia and Eastasia, and the three are constantly involved a series of shifting alliances and battles. Winston is a Party member, and wears the uniform of a Party member: blue overalls.

In the opening pages, we find Winston, having climbed the seven flights to his apartment slowly due to his bothersome varicose ankle ulcer, looking out his apartment window, noting the large and ominous presence of the four Ministry buildings: the Ministry of Truth, which manages news, entertainment, education and fine arts as related to the Party, the Ministry of Peace, which manages war, the Ministry of Love, which manages law and order, and the Ministry of Plenty, which manages economic affairs. In Newspeak, the official language of Oceania, these Ministries are referred to as Minitrue, Minipax, Miniluv, and Miniplenty. Winston sees the Ministry of Truth clearly from his apartment window, and can even make out the three Party slogans carved into the large, pyramid-shaped, glittering white concrete structure: "War is Peace," "Freedom is Slavery," and "Ignorance is Strength."

Winston's apartment contains a telescreen, an oblong metal plaque like a dulled mirror that simultaneously receives and transmits information. The machine constantly spews Party propaganda, but also monitors each Party member, listening to his or her words and observing his or her actions in search of evidence of disloyalty. The telescreens are an important tool of the Thought Police, whose sole responsibility is identifying those disloyal - even with a single word, phrase, or facial expression - to the Party. Strangely, the telescreen in Winston's apartment is hung at such an angle that there is a small alcove in which Winston cannot be seen. He sits at a desk in this alcove and begins to write in a diary he purchased discreetly from an antique shop. In 1984 Oceania, people do not keep personal documentation. Such behavior is considered dangerous, as it promotes independence and individual thought. In preparing to write in this diary, Winston knows he is committing thoughtcrime and therefore risking his life. Winston writes, "April 4th, 1984," and then realizes he is not even certain of the year, as it is impossible to tell if the information the Party disseminates is truly accurate anymore.

Winston begins writing about a violent war film with vivid death scenes. He then remembers an event from earlier in the day that inspired him to begin the diary. It occurred at about eleven hundred that morning (time is kept in the twenty-four hour method) during the Two Minutes Hate, a daily propaganda presentation given to groups at their places of work praising Big Brother, Oceania and the Party, and denouncing Emmanuel Goldstein, the figurehead of capitalism and the Party's number one enemy, and Oceania's current enemy of war. While surrounded by fellow Party members caught up in the fervor of denouncing enemies to the Party, literally screaming and throwing things at the screen and praising Big Brother and Oceania, Winston took note of those around him. He observed the dark-haired girl he had often seen in the Ministry who he hated based purely on her apparent worship of the Party, and also a man named O'Brien, an Inner Party member whom he also often saw in the Ministry of Truth. He and O'Brien made eye contact, and immediately Winston felt as though they were both thinking the same things, realizing that O'Brien also found this practice and the Party's propaganda disgusting. O'Brien, he suddenly understood, also yearned for individual freedoms. Bolstered by what he perceived to be nonverbal support of his anti-Party feelings, Winston resolved to begin his diary that day.

While remembering this event, Winston finds he has unknowingly written, DOWN WITH BIG BROTHER over and over in his diary. Winston feels slightly panicked, but then reminds himself that he knows he will be arrested: it is only a matter of time. A knock on the door interrupts his thoughts. Winston assumes that the Thought Police have already found him, but soon discovers that his visitor is Mrs. Parsons from across the hall. Her husband works with Winston at the Ministry of Truth, and Mrs. Parsons has come to ask Winston to help her unclog her sink. Winston obliges, and in doing so meets her son and daughter, who are both members of the Spies and Youth League, and ardent Party supporters, eager to display their loyalty. In fact, they are begging their mother to take them to the hanging of a declared enemy to the Party, an unfortunately common event. Winston predicts that quite soon these children will denounce their innocent parents to the Thought Police and be publicly named "child heroes."

Winston returns to his apartment and begins to reflect on the impossibility of escaping the Party. He begins thinking of O'Brien again, remembering how seven years ago he dreamt he was walking through a dark room, when he suddenly heard O'Brien's voice say, "We shall meet in the place where there is no darkness." Ever since that dream, Winston has increasingly understood O'Brien's shared perception of the Party. Moving on, he ponders the sacred principles of Ingsoc and the mutability of the past, and feels as though he is "wandering in the forests of the sea bottom, lost in a monstrous world where he himself was the monster." Winston feels alone in his internal rebellion and wonders for whom he is writing the diary. The chances of any human other than a member of the Thought Police ever reading his words is quite small. Before returning to work, Winston writes a few final thoughts in his diary: "From the age of uniformity, from the age of solitude, from the age of Big Brother, from the age of doublethink - greetings!" Finally, with solemn understanding, he notes, "Thoughtcrime does not entail death: thoughtcrime IS death." To be sure he is not discovered, Winston carefully washes the ink off his hands and places the diary in his desk drawer, complete with a noticeable piece of dust on the front cover - a security device that will reveal whether other hands have touched his precious book.

Analysis

In these first chapters of 1984, we meet the main character, Winston Smith, and learn about the totalitarian regime he lives under as a citizen of Airstrip One in Oceania. Winston lives a harsh and limited life: he is watched at every turn, and forced to submit to the Party in almost every aspect of his existence. In Oceania, those who do not submit to the Party suffer the wrath of the Thought Police. Orwell's parallels to totalitarian regimes of the early twentieth century such as Nazi Germany and Stalin's Soviet Union, and the degree of control they maintained over their citizens, are clear. In 1984, the Party maintains control over its citizens through the use of telescreens that transmit constant streams of propaganda while observing citizens, mandatory organized propaganda events such as the Two Minutes Hate and Hate Week, and by instilling the fear of the Thought Police and the retributions of thoughtcrime in all. The Party controls its citizens and maintains its power through the use of extensive psychological manipulation.

Winston views the regularities of his world - the face of Big Brother, the telescreen, the dilapidated apartment complex, and the sad existence of his neighbor and her Party-worshipping children - with sadness and disdain. He has deep reservations about the Party and believes there must be hope for a brighter future, in which personal freedoms are permitted. However, his neighbor's children's powerful allegiance to the Party scares Winston. He sees how young minds can be indoctrinated into the Party through organizations such as the Spies and the Youth League, which encourage children to report anyone they believe to be a thought criminal - even their parents - to the Party. This control and influence over the youngest members of Oceanian society speaks to the massive degree of psychological control the Party holds over its citizens, and again provides a parallel to similar totalitarian organizations of the twentieth century such as the Hitler Youth.

When we meet Winston, these rebellious notions have clearly been festering for quite some time. Now, in writing his diary, he is taking the first physical step towards all-out rebellion. In putting his pen to paper, Winston knows he is committing thoughtcrime. He is now a criminal, and knows that his eventual arrest is inevitable. This fatalistic perspective stays with Winston throughout the novel. As he often says to Julia, "We are the dead." He has no true hope for rebellion in his time, but he cannot submit to the Party. This in-between state forces him to constantly be reminded of his eventual arrest, torture, and death.

Winston is a unique citizen of Oceania. Although he was raised from an early age in the bosom of the Party, Winston harbors a strong sense of individual freedom, while those around him seem to soak in Party propaganda and find no fault with the Party's constant and seemingly obvious revisions of history. Through stressing the significance of Winston's risking his life through the physical act of writing, Orwell demonstrates the great rarity of personal freedom and self-expression in totalitarian regimes and clarifies the massive degree of control the Party holds over its citizens. At the same time, Winston's choice to begin the diary (and his subconsciously writing "DOWN WITH BIG BROTHER") shows us the strength of Winston's anti-Party feelings. Winston feels alone in his act of rebellion and his attitude towards the Party, but holds out hope that O'Brien shares his views. In these chapters we meet O'Brien, a man who becomes a symbol of rebellion in Winston's mind, for the first time. Ultimately, however, it is O'Brien who will guide Winston towards his downfall and will torture him into absolute submission.

Winston has vivid dreams that prove to be prophetic. Winston hears O'Brien's voice in a dream, telling him that they will "meet in the place where there is no darkness." They do eventually meet in this dream, but the "place where there is no darkness" is not associated with freedom as Winston had hoped. Rather, it is the interior of the Ministry of Love, where thought criminals such as Winston are tortured, and where the lights are always on. The irony in the naming of each ministry is an obvious notation on the contradictory nature of the Party. Criminals are tortured in the Ministry of Love, war is waged from the Ministry of Peace, misinformation and lies are regularly distributed from the Ministry of Truth, and the Ministry of Plenty oversees and manages the weak economy of Oceania, where most citizens live in poverty. In fact, London is in a serious state of urban decay, which the Party simply ignores, instead stating with a celebratory attitude how wonderful and plentiful the lives of Oceanian citizens are. The Party slogans exhibit similar contradictions: "War is Peace," "Freedom is Slavery," and "Ignorance is Strength." The Party is built and thrives upon such contradictions. Forcing acceptance of such blatant inaccuracies removes the individual's ability to question the Party or think independently.

# Summary and Analysis of Part One III-V

Winston dreams of his mother, who disappeared in one of the great purges of the 1950s, when Winston was ten or eleven years old. In his dream his mother is sitting below him with his baby sister in her arms, in some sort of underground room. In this memory, he feels sad because he knows that somehow she has given up her life and that of his sisters for him. He thinks of her death as a tragedy - impossible in current times, because she died loving him and giving herself up to a personal loyalty that current Party rule would never allow.

In his dream, Winston suddenly finds himself in the Golden Country, which he happens upon often in his slumbers. The Golden Country is an "an old rabbit-bitten pasture, with a foot track wandering across it and a molehole here and there...the elm trees were swaying faintly in the breeze, their leaves just stirring in dense masses like women's hair." In this dream, the dark-haired girl from the Ministry whom Winston despises for her Party-fueled fervor approaches him and tears off her clothes in a gesture so "splendid" that its existence alone rebels against the Party. He wakes with the word "Shakespeare" on his lips.

It is time for his morning Physical Jerks, an exercise routine implemented to all Party members through the telescreen, specifically tailored for each age group. Winston falls among the 30s to 40s group. After overcoming his daily morning coughing fit, Winston begins the exercise routine, but lets his mind wander to the history of Oceania. He can't remember a time when Oceania wasn't at war, but he remembers being quite young and rushing to an underground Tube station with his parents and little sister to take shelter during an attack - although he cannot remember the source of the attack. Next, he remembers an era of common London street fighting, and then only an era of permanent war. Winston remembers that only four years ago Oceania was at war with Eastasia, even though it is currently at war with Eurasia and claims this has always been the case. Such was the nature of doublethink - completely accepting the opposite of the known truth and adjusting one's personal memories accordingly. Winston realizes that the past has been not altered, but rather destroyed. Suddenly, a voice from the telescreen interrupts him, yelling out his name and identification number and urging him to "bend lower." Feigning interest and determination, Winston complies, and succeeds in touching his toes for the first time in many years.

At work in the Records Department of the Ministry of Truth, Winston reads his daily assignments, sent to him in the form of small cylindrical paper rolls that spurt out of a pneumatic tube. The messages order him to "rectify" certain articles or news items to ensure the Party is always proven right and good, no matter its original predictions and actual outcomes. For instance, the predictions of the Ministry of Plenty's output of goods need to be "rectified" to reflect recently-published "actual" numbers. Once Winston completes assignments by dictating corrections into the speakwrite at his desk (which translates spoken word into written word), Winston puts all related documentation into a "memory hole," thus sending any evidence of altered data to a large furnace in the center of the building.

When taking a short break from his work, Winston notices his coworker Tillotson sitting in the cubicle across from him, whispering secretively into his speakwrite and casting suspicious glances about the room. Winston realizes that he barely even knows the people in his department. The little he knows consists of workplace information and basic personal details. For instance, the sandy-haired woman in the cubicle next to him is responsible for tracking down and deleting all mention of any vaporized person, so as to remove their entire existence from the records. Ironically, her husband was vaporized not long ago. Ampleforth, a poet, sits a few cubicles away from Winston and produces "definitive texts," or garbled versions of poems that the Party has deemed ideologically offensive, but for some reason wants to retain. Winston then reflects on all the other departments in the Ministry of Truth, including those areas that create and distribute fiction, film, textbooks, and plays, both at the Party level and at a level specifically produced for the lower class non-Party members, the proletariat, or "proles," including Pornosec, which produces pornography that no Party member is allowed to even look at.

Returning to work, Winston admits that his greatest pleasure in life is his work. He is good at it, and although he despises the Party's reinvention of the past, he ironically takes pleasure in finding creative ways to complete particularly challenging assignments. Today, Winston creates a "Comrade Ogilvy" out of thin air to replace the name of a recently named "unperson," Inner Party member Comrade Withers, who once received the honor of the Order of Conspicuous Merit, Second Class. Winston creates an entire life for his fictional Comrade Ogilvy, and is sure his work will be found creative and satisfactory in solving the particularly difficult problem of removing a publicly-lauded Inner Party member from the records.

Winston enters the Ministry of Truth canteen and runs into Syme, whom he grudgingly calls his "friend." Syme is a Newspeak specialist working on the Eleventh Edition of the Newspeak Dictionary. The two men speak of the rarity of razor blades, and Winston lies, saying he has none, when he actually has a few saved at home for his personal use. Syme asks Winston why he didn't go to the hanging, suggests he knows that they make Winston uncomfortable, and then goes into grotesque detail about the event, noting how the man's tongue was bright blue and sticking out of his mouth when he died.

Winston and Syme obtain their bland, unrecognizable food, and sit. They begin to discuss the Newspeak dictionary, and Syme goes into great detail about his work, discussing the greatness he sees in the destruction of words and the simplification of language. For instance, why does a language need the word "bad," when "ungood" is sufficient? Syme claims that Oldspeak will be obsolete by the year 2050. Winston begins to say "Except for the proles," but cuts himself off as he realizes it might be unorthodox to make this claim. Despite this, Syme sees Winston's point and argues that he is wrong. In his opinion, Newspeak will take over completely, resulting in a climate without thought. He exclaims, "Orthodoxy means not thinking - not needing to think. Orthodoxy is unconsciousness." Upon hearing this statement, Winston thinks to himself that Syme is too intelligent, and will eventually be vaporized for seeing too clearly and speaking too plainly.

Tom Parsons eventually joins Winston and Syme. Parsons is an overweight, boyish, deeply loyal Party member with a very simple mind. He is quite active in Party activities and collects a subscription fee from Winston for the house by house Hate Week fund, which will be used to purchase flags and patriotic decorations for the event. Parsons apologizes to Winston for his son, who hit him with a toy catapult the other day, and then launches into a story about how his daughter followed a suspicious man during a troop hike and reported him to the authorities, claiming he was a foreigner because he was wearing "a funny kind of shoes." Winston is horrified, but outwardly agrees that she did her duty to the Party.

A telescreen announcement lauding the Ministry of Plenty's success in exceeding all production goals interrupts their conversation, and Winston reflects on the lies being told. He knows production did not meet the stated goals, but regardless of actual numbers, production will always be reported as far higher than expected. This supports Party morale and convinces the Party members that they are leading happy lives. The phrase "our new, happy life" is repeated often throughout the broadcast. In the midst of this announcement, Winston finds himself predicting the fates of those in his life. He believes that he, Mrs. Parsons, Syme, and O'Brien will be vaporized, while Parsons, the dark-haired girl, and other mindless followers of Party doctrine will never be subject to such a fate. Suddenly, he realizes that the dark-haired girl is staring at him. When he returns her gaze, she quickly looks away, and Winston begins to fear that she knows what he has been thinking and will report him for facecrime. Minutes later, Parsons tells another story of his children setting a woman's skirt on fire for having wrapped fish in newspaper containing pictures of Big Brother. A whistle blows, and the men return to work.

Analysis

Winston's prophetic dreams continue in this section. He dreams of the Golden Country, and of a sexual encounter with the dark-haired girl (whom we later learn is Julia). Later in the novel, this event actually takes place. This dark-haired girl is an object of sexual attraction for Winston, but also of hate. He is conflicted in his feelings for her, and represses both for fear of expressing himself too openly.

Throughout this section we clearly see the striking contradictions in the Party's constant revision of the past, which Winston directly contributes to through his position in the Records Department at the Ministry of Truth. Any past documentation challenging a current Party goal, achievement or development must be destroyed or altered to support the Party's current actions. In this way, the "past" is constantly changing, and constantly altered. At one point, Oceania is at war with Eurasia and *has always been* at war with Eurasia, but later in the novel, Oceania is at war with

Eastasia and *has always been* at war with Eastasia. For the Party, the past is mutable. Winston refuses to accept this, most visibly during the Ministry of Plenty report at the end of Chapter V where Winston listens in awe and disgust to false reports that the Ministry of Plenty has exceeded all production goals.

In detailing Winston's work life, Orwell reveals the inner workings of Party organizations and the fastidious control the Party wields over every detail of information administered to Party members and the masses. To work in the Ministry of Truth, Party members must embrace doublethink. They know they are altering past information, yet as loyal Party members must accept their own personal alterations as the truth. Winston cannot embrace doublethink. He knows the Party's version of the past is false - he remembers events the Party pretends never happened, and he refuses to ignore this knowledge.

Through a detailed account of Winston's work life, we also learn how lonely he is. He has no personal friends, except perhaps for Syme, whom he only grudgingly calls a friend. He observes the people he works among with a great deal of detachment. He knows little about their personal lives, and is generally frustrated by their simpleness. He tends to view them with disdain. This loneliness and separation from fellow mankind will fuel the intensity of Winston's eventual relationship with Julia and his longing for a friendship with O'Brien.

In these chapters, we also witness the degree of self-control Winston must wield in order to avoid discovery. In conversations with work colleagues, Winston stops himself from saying what he actually believes, and maintains great control over his facial expressions to avoid expressing discontent when it would be inappropriate to do so. Although Winston has become comfortable with this self-control, he doesn't trust himself completely. Therefore, when he catches the dark-haired girl looking at him during the Ministry of Plenty telescreen report, he is immediately worried that he has revealed himself, and that she will report him for facecrime.

# Summary and Analysis of Part One VI-VIII

Winston writes in his diary, revealing the details of a particularly sordid night when he had sex with a prole prostitute with a face thickly painted in makeup (which Party women never wear). Winston struggles with his internal turmoil surrounding this disdainful act, noting to himself that man's nervous system is his worst enemy. There is no way to fight involuntary facial spasms or talking in one's sleep. These are the actions that cannot be stopped, yet can condemn one to death.

Winston remembers his wife Katharine, whom he separated from but never divorced, as per Party practice. Winston describes how the Party works continually to remove all pleasure from sexual acts, seeing eroticism as an enemy. Party marriages must be approved by a committee, and to gain such approval, the man and woman in question must not demonstrate any true physical affection for one another. The goal of a marriage is to produce offspring, not to seek personal pleasure or satisfaction. In fact, certain Party organizations, including the Junior Anti-Sex League (of which the dark-haired girl is a member, as demonstrated by the crimson band around her waist), advocate celibacy and procreation through artsem, Newspeak for artificial insemination, and even suggest that children should be raised in public institutions rather than by parents.

Katharine and Winston separated almost eleven years ago, and Winston rarely thinks of her. He nicknamed her "the human soundtrack" because of her empty mind and willingness to spout Party propaganda. Katharine had always been extremely cold when it came to sex, but insisted that she and Winston must keep trying to have children so she could fulfill her "duty to the Party".

Winston returns to his story of prostitution, revealing that when he turned on the light to look at the nakedness of the woman he was about to have sex with, he realized that she was old. She had no teeth at all, and was at least fifty, but Winston completed the act nevertheless. In writing this admission, Winston struggles, pressing his fingers against his eyes and using every vestige of control to avoid screaming foul words.

Some time later, Winston writes, "If there is hope, it lies in the proles." The proles, who comprise eighty-five percent of Oceania's population, are the only ones, he believes, who can overthrow the Party. It is impossible to do so from within. Winston remembers walking down a street and hearing what he thought was a riot - a prole rebellion. In fact, it was women fighting over a limited supply of poorly made frying pans that broke in half during the scuffle. Winston writes, "Until they become conscious they will never rebel, and until after they have rebelled they cannot become conscious." Acknowledging this catch-22, Winston reflects on how the Party has claimed to have liberated the proles from the bondage and slavery of capitalist society, when in actuality the proles still live in squalor, work, produce children, drink beer, and die by age sixty. The Thought Police are always among them, seeking out those deemed too intelligent or too aware of the Party's activities, and removing them from society.

Winston takes a copy of a children's history textbook he obtained from Mrs. Parsons out of his desk drawer and begins to copy a passage describing the ills of capitalist society, including starving children having to work for cruel masters, and capitalist men always wearing long black coats with top hats. Winston then remembers other historical matters he has been taught about the capitalist past, including jus primae noctis, which supposedly was a "law by which every capitalist had the right to sleep with any woman working in one of his factories." Winston notes it is impossible to tell how many of these stories are lies, as nothing can be proved or disproved. Only once in his life has Winston ever held actual proof that Party history is false in his hands.

In the mid-sixties, during a series of great purges removing the original Revolutionary leaders, three men named Jones, Aaronson, and Rutherford were arrested. Under torture, they confessed to a variety of crimes. They were then released and returned to posts within the Party. Winston once saw them at the Chestnut Tree Cafe, and their spirits seemed entirely broken. While he observed them, a song came on over the telescreen: "Under the spreading chestnut tree, I sold you and you sold me..." Shortly afterwards, the three were rearrested and charged with a new string of crimes. Five years later, in 1973, Winston was at work and a newspaper clipping describing the three men at a function in New York on the date that they had confessed to being in Eurasia came into his workstation along with other rolled pieces of paper. Winston held in his hand concrete evidence of their innocence. Ten minutes later, Winston dropped the clipping into the memory hole, destroying it forever. But he never forgot the experience.

Remembering this day, Winston writes "I understand HOW: I do not understand WHY." He wonders if he is alone in this belief that the Party alters history, sometimes for entirely unknown reasons. He wonders if he is a lunatic, and whether it is possible to know that anything is true. Recalling O'Brien's face, he realizes he is sane. With new courage, he writes, "Freedom is the freedom to say that two plus two make four. If that is granted, all else follows."

After work one night, Winston finds himself wandering through the streets of London, among the proles. After being warned, he survives a "steamer" (rocket bomb) attack, a common occurrence in London, which constantly suffers such attacks. Following the attack, he continues his walk and finds himself near the antique shop where he bought his diary and the stationary shop where he bought his pen and ink. Across the street, he sees a very old man enter a pub and decides to take the risk of following him in and asking him about life before the Revolution.

In the pub, the old man keeps asking the bartender for a "pint," and the frustrated bartender keeps explaining to him that there are only liters and half-liters for sale. He does not know what a "pint" is. Winston buys the man a drink and begins to ask him pointed questions about the past and how things have changed since the Revolution. The man acknowledges living before the Revolution, but only refers to life before the Revolution with references to minute details of his life that Winston does not find particularly interesting or satisfying, such as references to top hats, lackeys, and his luck with women. The man simply does not answer Winston as to whether life was better before or after the Revolution.

Frustrated, Winston leaves and finds himself in front of the antique shop. He walks in, thinking he can claim that he is looking for razor blades if he is questioned. The owner of the store, Mr. Charrington, is a frail man of about sixty years old with benevolent eyes, thick spectacles, white hair, and bushy eyebrows. Winston notes that he has a "vague air of intellectuality" about him. The man remembers when he was last in the store, buying the rare diary, or, as he calls it, the "young lady's keepsake album." Winston wanders through the shop and finds a paperweight with a piece of coral inside of it. Winston is struck by its beauty and decides to purchase it. Mr. Charrington suggests that Winston take a look at another room, above the shop. The room consists of a strip of carpet, a few pictures, an armchair, a fireplace, an old-fashioned twelve-hour clock, and a large bed. With amazement, Winston realizes that there is no telescreen. The man explains that he never had a need for one, and begins to show Winston a picture on the wall of St. Clement's Dane. He recites part of a nursery rhyme about the old church: "Oranges and lemons, say the bells of St. Clement's...You owe me three farthings, say the bells of St. Martin's" He cannot remember the rest of it, but knows that the rhyme included the names of all the London churches.

Winston eventually extricates himself from Mr. Charrington and leaves the shop. He wanders home, briefly wondering what it might be like to rent the upper room from the old man. While recalling the rhyme Mr. Charrington shared, he suddenly sees the dark-haired girl from the Ministry of Truth on the road in front of him. In a panic, he stands stock still as she quickly walks on. He wanders aimlessly for a few minutes and then stops, wondering if he should turn back, follow the girl, and murder her with the paperweight to prevent himself from being turned in to the Thought Police. He quickly abandons the idea, thinking himself too weak, and heads home. Once back in his apartment, he chides himself for being so fearful and not acting to protect himself. He writes the rhyme down in his diary and begins contemplating what will happen to him when the Thought Police do eventually come to take him away. He will be tortured; his bones will snap; he will bleed and scream in pain. He thinks of O'Brien saying, "We will meet in the place with no darkness." In his train of thought the image of Big Brother merges and then replaces that of O'Brien. He pulls a coin from his pocket to look at the face of Big Brother, and is instead confronted with the Party slogans: "War is Peace," "Freedom is Slavery," and "Ignorance is Strength."

Analysis

Through Winston's painful memory of his experience with an aged prole prostitute, we begin to understand the depths of the Party's sexual repression. The memory pains Winston. Because he was so desperate for a close sexual experience, he continued the encounter even after realizing that the heavily made up woman was toothless and old. The Party represses all sexual acts in an effort to force Party members to channel all of their energy into furthering its own goals and needs. The Party must approve all marriages, and such unions must not appear to be sought because of sexual attraction. Sexual pleasure is an individual act, promoting independent thought and independent experiences. Clearly, sex is required for procreation, but through organizations such as the Junior Anti-Sex League, the Party turns sex into a duty performed purely to continue the Party and propagate the human race rather than an act performed for personal pleasure. Winston's wife Katharine felt this way, and was frigid in the bedroom, much to Winston's frustration and humiliation. As we later learn, the Party even encourages abstinence and advocates procreation only through artificial insemination.

The children's textbook (undoubtedly published in the Ministry of Truth) Winston has obtained is particularly revealing of the Party's revisionist history. The Party demonizes capitalism and capitalists, and Winston does not know what information in the book is true and what is false. Winston's story of the newspaper clipping proving Jones, Aaronson, and Rutherford's innocence further evidences the degree to which he yearns for information about the past. Although Winston destroyed the clipping, he knows that it existed, and he knows that the Party covered it up. Here, he addresses an important question that will continue to arise throughout the novel, and will only be answered in the Ministry of Love: Why? He understands how the Party revises history, but does not understand why this constant revision is necessary.

When Winston travels out into the prole world, we begin to see how the rest of the Oceanian population lives. The proles are destitute, living in poverty in areas removed from Party business and life. The prole areas are also the only places Winston and the others can go if they wish to find relics of the past. Winston notably visits Mr. Charrington's antique store, purchases a paperweight, and dreams about what it might be like to live in the apartment above the shop, free from the eyes of a telescreen. Winston is in awe of Mr. Charrington's shop, and wishes he could soak in the history of his artifacts. Winston sees great freedom in the prole world, and it is for this reason that be believes that if there is hope, "it lies with the proles." Unfortunately, the proles seem unable to capitalize on their freedoms, and take no interest in Party affairs.

When Winston meets the old man in the bar, we see the stark contrast between his hopes for a prole rebellion and the reality of prole existence. Winston hopes that the old man will reveal ideological differences between life before the Revolution and life under Party control. However, the man focuses only on very personal memories that do not speak to Winston's concerns. Winston becomes frustrated in this conversation because he believes that the proles, who are not subjected to doublethink and the revision of history, hold the true details of history, and therefore the hope for a brighter future.

When visiting Mr. Charrington, Winston sees the picture of St. Clement's Dane for the first time. This picture, and its accompanying rhyme, become symbols of the past for Winston. He holds onto this picture, and to the first few lines of the rhyme that Mr. Charrington remembered, believing that they represent his ideal of incontrovertible truth and rebellion against the Party. The Party cannot control this picture, or this poem. Despite the hope Winston places in this object and this rhyme, both foreshadow his downfall. The rhyme ends with the line, "Here comes a chopper to chop off your head," and much later we will learn that a telescreen is hidden behind the picture. Winston's walk through this prole area of the city further confirms his rebellion, and continues to set him on the path towards eventual arrest and defeat.

# Summary and Analysis of Part Two I-III

In the middle of the morning, Winston takes a break from working to go to the bathroom. He notices the dark-haired girl walking towards him. The two are alone in the hallway. The girl falls, and Winston rushes to help her up. While assisting her, she discreetly hands him a small piece of paper. To avoid detection, he waits five minutes at his desk before allowing himself to read it, all the time imagining that perhaps it is a warning or a summons from the Thought Police. Finally he looks at it. It reads, "I love you." Winston is stunned.

At home in bed, Winston is able to think about the paper and work through his feelings. He tries to determine how to get in touch with the girl to arrange a rendezvous. Because she works in the Fiction Department, it would be too obvious if they ran into each other again in the hallway. For the next week, they keep missing each other in the canteen. Finally, he manages to sit an otherwise vacant table, only a few seats away from her. Speaking in near whispers, and not looking at each other, they quickly agree to meet at Victory Square.

In Victory Square, the excitement of a convoy of Eurasian prisoners causes a crowd, and they are able to stand side to side. The girl takes charge of the conversation immediately, outlining a plan to meet in a specific and distant point in the country that Sunday afternoon. Winston agrees. Just before the crowd parts the girls squeezes his hand, and upon touching it Winston feels he has learned every part of it by heart.

On Sunday, Winston travels into the country, following the girl's directions. While he is picking her some wildflowers, she finds him and they head to the secluded spot she has in mind. Before anything happens, Winston tells the girl that he is thirty-nine, and has varicose veins, a wife, and five false teeth. The girl replies that she does not care. They begin talking, and Winston learns that the girl's name is Julia. She has known for some time that he is Winston Smith. Winston reveals that he believed Julia to be part of the Thought Police. Julia finds such a notion quite funny, but appears to take some pleasure in being that believable as a Party devotee.

Julia and Winston stroll through the little enclave. Winston, standing at the edge of their small clearing, suddenly recognizes the scenery: it is the Golden Country from his dreams. A small thrush perched near them begins to sing passionately, and the sound strikes Winston as an example of simple, pure, unstoppable beauty. They head back to the clearing. Just as he saw in his dream, Julia tears off her clothes and they embrace. She reveals that she has done this with many Party members, and Winston explains that the more men she has been with, the more he will love her. He is inspired by her freedom and passionate rebellion, as corruption within the Party gives him hope for the future. After having sex, Winston likens their affair to a political act; a blow against the Party.

When Julia wakes from her short slumber, she immediately becomes businesslike:

she dresses herself, and discusses where they should next meet, as it is dangerous to return to the same place more than a couple of times. They are able to meet up again privately once in the month of May, in a ruined church belfry, but otherwise they must be satiated with minor, seemingly accidental and unnoticed encounters in public streets, during which they pretend not to know each other. At the church tower, Winston learns more about Julia's life. She is twenty-six, lives in a hostel with other girls, and works on the novel-writing machine in the Fiction Department. She has no memories of life before the Revolution, and knows barely anyone who does. Throughout her life she has been an ideal Party member, often singled out for leadership roles in youth organizations. She also reveals that she has worked in Pornosec, the pornography section of the Fiction Department, devoted to creating pornographic stories for the proles. Apparently the Party believes women are better suited for Pornosec, because their morals won't be as tempted by the material as their male counterparts'. She had her first love affair at sixteen, and does not believe in the underground anti-Party Brotherhood movement.

Winston discusses his own life, and talks about his wife, Katharine, calling her "goodthinkful," meaning entirely and completely loyal to the Party, even in her most private thoughts. Winston hated her, and her cold, businesslike approach to their sex life. Julia predicts that Katharine called sex her "duty to the Party," and Winston is surprised to learn that this is a phrase women are taught to use. With this realization, he begins to understand the depths of the Party's sexual Puritanism. Removing sex allows one's energy to be otherwise focused, into violent loyalty to the Party and hatred of its enemies. Moreover, removing the parent instinct removes any loyalty other than that to the Party. Next, Winston reveals that once, while separated from a larger group on a walk in the country, he considered murdering his wife, but did not. Julia states that he should have done it to free himself. Winston agrees.

After a moment, Winston begins to understand that Julia believes it might be possible to continue living a secret life, while Winston knows the Thought Police will find them eventually. Stating his belief, Winston says, "We are the dead." Julia argues that they are not dead yet and begins to describe her next plan for them to meet.

Analysis

In these chapters, Winston takes a significant step in his rebellion against the Party. He begins a love affair, blatantly rejecting the Party's hatred of sexual attraction and enjoyment. In Julia, Winston finally finds a compatriot in his quest against the Party. He is no longer alone. Julia's presence supports Winston's anti-Party thoughts and feelings, but their affair also highlights the differences in their attitudes toward the Party. Julie despises the Party, but accepts it as a permanent ruling government. She has no illusions of bringing the Party down or of a successful rebellion against it. Rather, she enjoys finding her own ways to rebel against the Party, such as efficiently planning her and Winston's encounters. Julia wants to live as long as possible without being caught in her small rebellions, and within the bounds of the

Party. In contrast, Winston is sure that he will be arrested and will die. Rather than working to protect his own life, Winston embraces fatalism while holding out hope for a rebellion against the Party and dreams of a Party-free future.

Julia and Winston meet in the square and observe a procession of prisoners of war. Here, we see the brutality of the totalitarian regime. The Party purposely parades these prisoners through a public square to use them as sources of propaganda and to rally the crowd against them. The parade of prisoners suggests that the Party is succeeding in battle and rallies the crowd's support for the Party's war efforts. Here again, the Party is masterfully manipulating the minds of its subjects through carefully planned propaganda efforts. Moreover, these prisoners and others already in Oceania are the only foreigners in the nation. Oceanian citizens never interact with foreigners - yet another method of control that prevents Oceanian citizens from understanding what life would be like outside of Oceania or beyond the reach of the Party. With no basis for comparison, Oceanian citizens have no choice but to be content with their lives.

Winston and Julia's encounter in the Golden Country is an important moment in the novel. Here, Winston sees the vision from his dream - Julia ripping her clothes of in the middle of the Golden Country - transformed into reality. In addition, he is inspired by a thrush's passionate song, which is, in Winston's eyes, a wonderful expression of freedom and beauty. Throughout the novel, Winston finds great inspiration in music. Here, it is through the thrush, and in much of the rest of the novel, it is through the red-armed, large prole woman who sings passionately while doing laundry in her yard.

Winston talks about his wife with Julia, revealing her sexual frigidity, and Julia is not surprised. Again, the Party's puritanical views on sexuality become apparent. Winston is encouraged to learn that Julia has had many affairs, her first at age sixteen. In his eyes, this behavior is a great act of political rebellion against the Party, and he is eager to take part in it. On a more personal level, Winston is elated to finally be in a sexual relationship where both parties are eager for personal pleasure, and in which the Party plays no role.

# Summary and Analysis of Part Two IV-VII

Winston stands in the room above Mr. Charrington's shop, looking around. His paperweight is on the small desk, and the room now contains a small oil stove, a saucepan, and two pots, all supplied by Mr. Charrington. Winston rented the room from Mr. Charrington, clearly for a love affair with Julia. Rather than judging him, Mr. Charrington noted vaguely that privacy was very valuable these days. Winston hears someone singing beneath his window. He looks out and sees a large, stocky prole woman hanging baby diapers, singing, "It was only an 'opless fancy..." Apparently, this is a Party song published for the benefit of the proles, who revel in machine-generated verse.

Winston admits to himself that he has taken a great risk in renting the room, but remembers how hard it had been for he and Julia to meet. Once, she had to cancel a planned reunion because her menstrual cycle was early. At first Winston was furious, but upon recognizing the depth of their bond was calmed by a powerful wave of tenderness towards Julia. His mind wanders to their eventual arrest and what awaits them in the Ministry of Love, but Julia's entrance interrupts his dismal reverie.

Julia has brought with her many black market items, including good bread, real coffee, sugar, makeup, and perfume. When she puts on the makeup and allows Winston to see her, he is pleased. Julia reveals her plan to get a real dress and a pair of silk stockings so that - in Mr. Charrington's apartment, at least - she can be a woman rather than a Party member, and embrace her femininity. Winston and Julia make love on the large bed and sleep for a short time. When they wake, Julia sees a rat poking his head out of a corner of the room. Winston is horrified, revealing that he is more afraid of rats than anything else: "Of all the horrors in the world - a rat!" Winston remembers his recurring nightmare of standing in front of a wall of darkness, knowing that on the other side lies something dreadful.

Julia explores the room, noting the paperweight and the picture on the wall. Winston tells her of Mr. Charrington's poem, and she adds to it: "You owe me three farthings say the bells of St. Martin's / When will you pay me, say the bells of Old Bailey?" Winston is shocked, but Julia reveals that her grandfather, who lived before the war and was vaporized, used to recite it to her. Julia begins to get dressed and clean up, while Winston picks up his paperweight and imagines that his life inside this apartment is like the coral: trapped inside thick, safe, protective crystal, fixed in eternity.

It is some weeks later, and Syme has vanished. Just as Winston predicted, Syme has been vaporized. His name has been deleted from Ministry records, and people begin to behave as though they never knew him. Winston has been working long hours to prepare for Hate Week. The weather has become hot, and the population seems eager for activity: they hang banners, posters and signs, and proudly sing the Hate Song. In the lead-up to Hate Week, Winston has noticed a new, particularly large poster of a

Eurasian soldier wielding a machine gun all over the city. Winston and Julia continue to meet in the apartment above Mr. Charrington's shop, dealing with its meager amenities and apparent bug problem in order to revel in their increasing happiness. Winston's ulcer has subsided, his coughing fits have disappeared, and his anger has somewhat abated. He has begun regularly chatting with Mr. Charrington about old times and the things in the shop. The apartment has become a refuge where he feels safe from the Party, able to act as a person rather than a Party member. However, Winston still understands - albeit distantly - that his fate is sealed. Such rebellion will not go unnoticed forever. Their time is precious.

Winston tells Julia of the bond he feels with O'Brien, and she understands why Winston might recognize him as sympathetic to his feelings. Julia believes deeply in the power of such relationships, but also tends to assume that most people are fundamentally against the Party, even though she doubts the existence of the Brotherhood. Although she is rebellious, Julia is somewhat naive in Winston's eyes. She believes that the Party invented the airplane, barely understands who Goldstein was, and cannot remember that Oceania was once at war with Eastasia (rather than Eurasia). The ease with which she accepts the Party's propaganda slightly disturbs Winston.

While walking through a hallway at work, Winston hears a small cough behind him. He turns and sees O'Brien, and feels that finally the day has come when he will receive a message from the Brotherhood. O'Brien begins the conversation by claiming that he knows Winston is interested in Newspeak, even vaguely referring to Syme, who was recently vaporized. O'Brien offers Winston an advance copy of the Tenth Edition of the Newspeak Dictionary and gives Winston his home address so that he can come pick up the copy. Then, as suddenly as he arrived, O'Brien is gone. Winston reflects on the interaction, believing that he is taking yet another step towards complete rebellion, and towards his own grave.

Winston and Julia are in Mr. Charrington's apartment. Winston wakes with eyes full of tears. He tells Julia that he has been dreaming of his mother. He remembers that shortly after his father disappeared, he lived with his mother and his baby sister. Times were difficult, air raids were common, and rations were small. Winston's mother was highly distraught. She performed all her household duties, but rarely spoke, and sometimes held Winston for inexplicably long periods of time. Winston was a selfish young boy who always demanded more food from his mother even though there was barely enough for them to share, and sometimes even stole from his little sister's plate. One day, Winston's mother broke apart the two-ounce chocolate ration, giving three quarters to Winston and one quarter to his little sister. Winston snatched his sister's piece and ran from the house, his mother screaming for him to come back. He never saw her again. When he returned to the apartment several hours later, his mother and sister were gone.

After Winston tells his story, Julia responds by saying that she bets he was "a beastly little swine" in those days. Winston tries to explain the point of the story, but Julia falls asleep. He thinks of a violent propaganda movie he saw in which a refugee mother in a small boat tried to protect her son from a bomb by wrapping her arm around him. He finds a similarity between her gesture and his memories of his mother. Both women cared first for their children, and only second for their Party or their country. Such personal loyalty does not exist anymore. The Party has destroyed it by removing the sex instinct and family bonds. Winston realizes that the proles maintain these loyalties, and discovers a newfound respect for them. He says aloud, "The proles are human beings. We are not human." Julia wakes, and they begin discussing their relationship and what will happen when they are arrested. They agree that the Party will never be able to force them to stop loving each other. Staying human and maintaining their love is the ultimate rebellion against the Party.

Analysis

In these chapters, Winston and Julia settle into their affair. Winston takes another significant step towards his eventual arrest by renting Mr. Charrington's room. Originally he rejects the notion, understanding that to rent the apartment will definitely mean death. However, his love for Julia and their agreed-upon hatred of the Party emboldens him, and he decides to take the risk. When Julia sees the room, she is satisfied. She adds a line to the St. Clement's Dane poem, which thrills Winston. She also suggests cleaning the St. Clement's Dane picture, but never does. If she had, perhaps she and Winston would have discovered the telescreen hiding underneath and avoided arrest.

The paperweight Winston bought from Mr. Charrington earlier on takes on a larger symbolic meaning in these chapters. Just as the painting of St. Clement's Dane and its accompanying rhyme hold special meaning for Winston, so does the paperweight. One day after Julia leaves the apartment, Winston imagines he and Julia living in a world inside the paperweight, protected by the beautiful glass and removed from any sense of time or place. The paperweight, the apartment, the picture of St. Clement's Dane and its accompanying rhyme all symbolize Winston's hopes for freedom, yet are all false symbols. Each is obtained from Mr. Charrington, who is later revealed to be a member of the Thought Police. Even in what Winston believes is his path towards a greater understanding of the Party, history, reality, and the potential for rebellion, he is being manipulated by the Party. Perhaps the only real thing in his life is Julia. She came to him independently of the Party, and their love is the single act of rebellion that is not defined or controlled by the Party.

The prole woman singing outside the apartment window is another important symbol introduced in these chapters. Winston has already revealed a near-obsession with the proles and a belief that if there is hope, "it lies with the proles." As such, he takes a strong interest in the large, sturdy prole woman who sings simple yet passionate songs while hanging her laundry. In the prole woman, Winston recognizes a zest for life that Party members never enjoy. Listening to her songs and watching her work inspires Winston. She makes him believe that there is hope for humanity outside of the Party, perhaps in the next generation of proles.

In the apartment, Winston reveals his biggest fear: rats. When Julia points out one that is trying to sneak into the room through a hole in the corner, Winston is terrified. He describes a vague nightmare he has always had where a large wall prevents something horrible from reaching him. In the dream he never sees what is behind the wall, but in his mind he knows it is a horde of rats. Here again, Winston's dreams prove quite important to his waking life. Later, in the Ministry of Love, O'Brien will capitalize on this fear to break the last vestiges of Winston's independence and loyalty to Julia. Horrified at the idea of a rat cage being locked onto his face, Winston finally betrays his love.

In this section, Winston learns that his "friend" Syme has been vaporized. Syme is the first character in the novel to be vaporized, and his disappearance drives home the very real threat of arrest and death. Winston is headed down a similar path, but he cannot stop himself. Although death is inevitable, Winston forges on, again embracing his fatalistic outlook.

In this section, Winston finally meets and speaks to O'Brien, who has long been a symbol of the potential for rebellion from within the Party. The meeting is everything Winston had hoped for. O'Brien approaches him and gives him his address, an action Winston immediately recognizes as an invitation to discuss the Brotherhood. He thinks that the moment has finally come: he will join the rebellion, and his life will take on meaning. Tragically, we will later learn that Winston is wrong and that O'Brien is laying a trap.

In waking from a dream in which Winston remembers the last time he ever saw his mother, we begin to understand the suffering Winston endured as a child and the guilt he has carried over his mother and sister's deaths. Winston is deeply pained by the selfish acts of his childhood, and remembers his mother's love for his sister and for himself. Winston begins to understand that before the Party, loyalty to family came before loyalty to the Party. When Winston recognizes this sentiment in a Party propaganda film, he finds hope that somewhere in the world there are people who love each other. Such humanity, which Winston and Julia exhibit in their love, must mean that the potential exists to overthrow the Party. Once again, we see Winston and Julia's love as an act of rebellion in and of itself. They agree that the Party will never be able to destroy their love, and in that way, they are above the power of the Party. Once again, we will later learn that they are wrong in this assumption, and that the Party can indeed break their spirits and their love.

# Summary and Analysis of Part Two VIII-X

Winston and Julia, having traveled by different routes, arrive at O'Brien's apartment. Winston is nervous to have even entered the rich, spacious part of town that the Inner Party members live in, which smells of rare foods and tobacco. O'Brien's servant, Martin, is dark-haired, has a diamond-shaped face Winston believes to be Chinese, and wears a crisp white jacket. Martin brings Winston and Julia to O'Brien. O'Brien's flat is luxurious, with thick blue carpeting and clean, cream-colored walls. Before greeting his visitors, O'Brien completes a brief bit of business. Winston suddenly wonders if he is welcome, and whether he should have come. He has no proof that O'Brien is a member of a political conspiracy against the Party. He is acting only on glances, brief conversations, and a feeling in his gut.

O'Brien walks over to his guests, switching off his telescreen on his way. Winston and Julia are astounded. They never knew anyone who had the power to turn off a telescreen. O'Brien explains that Inner Party members have that privilege. The three face each other for a moment, and O'Brien asks, "Shall I say it or will you?" Winston launches into an admission of thoughtcrime, his and Julia's hatred of Big Brother and the Party, and their belief in and eagnerness to join the underground movement. Martin appears with refreshments, which turn out to be wine, something Winston and Julia have never tasted. O'Brien explains that Martin is "one of us" and asks him to sit with them.

O'Brien answers Winston's questions, explaining that Goldstein is real and that the Brotherhood (the anti-Party movement) exists. He then asks Winston and Julia what they are willing to do for the cause. They claim that they are willing to do anything, including murdering innocents and committing suicide, to further the Brotherhood. The only thing that they are unwilling to do is to part and never see each other again. O'Brien sends Martin to the pantry and begins to lecture Winston and Julia, explaining to them that they must obey him no matter what his instructions, and that he must effectively keep them in the dark about the extent of the underground organization so as to keep other members safe from discovery. Once the Thought Police find them, the Brotherhood will abandon Winston and Julia to protect the cause. Winston and Julia watch O'Brien with a sense of wonder and deep respect, and Winston believes that O'Brien represents hope for mankind. Before sending Julia out, O'Brien calls for a toast. Winston offers, "To the past," and they drink. Julia leaves, and O'Brien and Winston begin to speak of logistics. Winston reveals his "hiding place," Mr. Charrington's shop, and O'Brien tells him he will send him a copy of "the book...Goldstein's book." One day in the near future, Winston will find a misprint on an assignment and will have to ask for a repeat. The next day, he is to leave his briefcase at home. At some point during the day a man will walk up to him saying, "I believe you dropped your briefcase," and give him a briefcase containing the book. Before Winston and O'Brien part, O'Brien again offers a toast, saying "We shall meet again - if we do not meet again..." Winston interrupts hesitantly, stating, "We shall meet in the place of no darkness?" O'Brien agrees. Asked if he has any more questions before he leaves, Winston questions O'Brien about the rhyme Mr. Charrington taught him. O'Brien reveals the rest of the poem, adding, "When I grow rich, say the bells of Shoreditch." The poem is complete. The men shake hands, and Winston leaves.

Winston is walking towards Mr. Charrington's apartment, carrying "the book" and feeling utterly exhausted. He has worked more than ninety hours in five days, along with everyone else in the Party, because of Hate Week. On the sixth day, the enemy changed from Eurasia to Eastasia. Immediately, all the propaganda had to be adjusted to denounce Eastasia rather than Eurasia, Oceania's new ally. Winston recalls that when the event happened, he was watching a speech. The speaker was interrupted and after reading the newsflash, continued on almost seamlessly, denouncing Eastasia rather than Eurasia, which he had been discussing only moments before. The Party worked to "correct" old news stories and propaganda about being at war with Eurasia. In the view of the Party, Oceania had always been at war with Eastasia.

Finally, Winston reaches the apartment, sits on the bed, and opens the book. He reads the title page: "The Theory and Practices of Oligarchical Collectivism by Emmanuel Goldstein." Winston begins to read. The book opens with a discussion of basic class levels. Winston decides to jump ahead and begins reading the third chapter, which discusses how the world was split into three super powers. Russia absorbed Europe, and the United States absorbed Great Britain. A decade later, after a great deal of fighting, Eastasia finally solidified. Eurasia consists of the whole,

> "northern part of the European and Asiatic land mass, from Portugal to the Bering Strait, Oceania comprises the Americas, the Atlantaic islands including the British Isles, Australasia, and the souther portion of Africa. Eastasia, smaller than the other and with a less definite western frontier, comprises China and the countries to the south of it, the Japanese islands and a large but fluctuating portion of Manchuria, Mongolia, and Tibet."

Goldstein explains that for the past twenty-five years, these superstates have been permanently at war, despite the impossibility of a decisive outcome. Goldstein claims that the goal of modern warfare is to use the products created by society without raising standards of living. When a war is on, massive production is needed, but economic growth is impossible. The superstate populations are kept "bare, hungry, and dilapidated," compared to how they lived before the Revolution.

Goldstein notes the difficulty in maintaining a balance between wealth and power in healthy, growing societies. He explains that it was perceived that the only way to strike an effective balance and make all members of society equals would be to quickly distribute goods to prevent consumer growth: "The essential act of War is destruction." Scientists no longer pursue knowledge alone. Rather, they study facial expressions to determine ways to detect thoughtcrime, or chemistry to develop new weapons. Goldstein even notes that there has been very little development in weaponry. Each country still builds and hoards atomic bombs, which were developed long before the superstates were established.

Oceania is ruled under the ideology of Ingsoc, Eurasia under Neo-Bolshevism, and Eastasia under what can be translated as either "Death-worship" or "Obliteration of the Self." All countries have an Inner Party, a Party, a prole structure, and worship absolute, semi-divine leaders. Goldstein states, "when war becomes literally continuous, it also ceases to be dangerous...technical progress can cease and the most palpable facts can be denied or disregarded." The people have no way of knowing the true state of the world, and must rely entirely upon the Party. Rather than being a war between nations, the war is waged upon the people to maintain loyalty, unity against a common enemy, and Party domination. Thus, as war maintains order in each individual nation, the meaning of the Party slogan "War is Peace" becomes clear.

Julia arrives, briefly acknowledges the book, and busies herself making coffee. Half an hour later, while lying in bed, Winston tells Julia she must also read the book, and she asks him to read it aloud so that they can both take it in at the same time. He begins again at the first chapter.

Goldstein discusses the pyramidal shape of society, which consists of the High, who wish to remain high, Middle, who wish to change places with the high, and Low, who wish to develop a society based on equality among all men. When the Middle works to overthrow the High, it enlists the Low to achieve its goals, and then pushes the Low back to their place. Thus, the Low are always trod upon, with no hope of true change or progress. This pattern became clear in the nineteenth century, when Socialism began to gain popularity. The socialist movements among the superstates turned into totalitarian rule, which eventually evolved into Ingsoc, Neo-Bolshevism, and Death-worship, and worked directly towards developing "unfreedom and inequality." The purpose of these systems was to stop progress and "freeze history at a chosen moment." Rather than moving forward, society moved backward, embracing concepts such as "imprisonment without trial, the use of war prisoners as slaves, public executions [and] torture." Goldstein blames the invention of the television for the complete loss of privacy and the drastic increase in domestic spying. The television and propagation of print media allows superstates to develop and maintain complete uniformity in opinion.

Goldstein defines the four dangers to a ruling regime as being conquered from without, suffering from inefficient government leading to revolt, permitting a strong and independent Middle Group to develop, or losing self-confidence and willingness to govern. The main danger lies in the growth of liberalism. To address this, the government works efficiently to mold consciousness. As such, the infallible, all-powerful Big Brother sits at the apex of Oceanian society, as a representation of the Party to its country and the world, and "a focus point for love, fear, and reverence, emotions which are more easily felt toward an individual than toward an organization." Next lies the Inner Party, numbering approximately six million, less than two percent of the population. The Outer Party follows, filled with workers who allow the Party to maintain society, and finally come the proles, the "dumb masses" and non-Party members consisting of eighty-five percent of the population. Membership in these groups is defined by heredity, and each is monitored closely by the Thought Police to weed out any independent thinkers.

Goldstein goes on to discuss the advent of Newspeak, the total lack of privacy demanded by the Party, and the central notion of the mutability of the past. Goldstein focuses specifically on the Newspeak word "doublethink," which means "the power of holding two contradictory beliefs in one's mind simultaneously, and accepting both of them." Goldstein notes that the Party tends to embrace contradiction, "constantly linking opposites - knowledge with ignorance, cynicism with fanaticism," peace with war, truth with lies, plenty with starvation, love with torture. In this way, the Party has abandoned every basic principle of Socialism and turned its back on the original goals of the Revolution.

Winston stops reading and realizes that Julia has fallen asleep. He lies down next to her, noting that he still has not learned the "ultimate secret." He knows *how*, but not *why*. He knew all of these things before, but reading Goldstein's words showed him that he was sane. He falls asleep murmuring, "Sanity is not statistical."

Winston wakes thinking that he has slept for a long time, but the clock suggests otherwise. He hears the deep singing of the prole woman in the yard below. Julia wakes and notices that the oil stove is empty, which is strange considering she had been sure to fill it. Julia dresses, and they take a moment to observe the prole woman in her yard, performing her domestic duties and thriving in her simple life. Winston calls her beautiful, and reflects on how she must have changed quite quickly from a young, supple beauty to a hardened, wide mother of many needy children. He thinks about all the people in the world who live similarly simple lives, focused on family, children, and daily work, and again tells himself that if there is hope, it lies in the proles. He knows that this must have been Goldstein's conclusion as well, and takes heart in the notion that eventually "strength would change into consciousness," and humanity would recapture the earth. In comparing himself to the freedom of the proles, he states aloud, "We are the dead." Julia echoes his words, and then suddenly, a voice from behind them states, "You are the dead." Winston and Julia jump apart in fear. Julia realizes that the voice is coming from behind the picture. The voice tells them to stay where they are, and then adds the final lines to the St. Clement's poem, "Here comes a candle to light you to bed / Here comes a chopper to chop off your head!" The picture falls to the ground, revealing a hidden telescreen. The Thought Police break in through the window, smash Winston's coral paperweight to the ground, and hit Julia. Mr. Charrington walks into the room, and Winston realizes that he looks younger, taller, colder, and more alert. He suddenly realizes that it was Mr. Charrington's voice on the telescreen; Mr. Charrington is a member of the Thought Police.

Analysis

Finally, Winston and Julia meet O'Brien in his home to discuss rebellion against the Party. This pivotal moment places Winston and Julia - in their minds, at least - forever on a path towards rebellion, but in reality only sends them careening towards arrest and torture. Winston's easy admission of hatred for the Party and desire to join an underground organization working against it seals his eventual downfall, but frees his spirit. Winston believes that he has finally found the anti-Party organization he has sought throughout his life. Throughout the meeting, both Winston and Julia are in awe of O'Brien's simultaneous status as a member of the Inner Party position and dedication to the Party's destruction. In expressing great confidence, knowledge and power, O'Brien is further established as a man of great wisdom and knowledge. Winston references his dream when he closes a toast with O'Brien, saying they shall meet "in the place where there is no darkness." Before leaving, Winston asks O'Brien about the St. Clement's Dane rhyme, and O'Brien is symbolically able to complete the verse, which assures Winston of O'Brien's like-mindedness. As is sadly common in Winston's experience, we later learn that O'Brien has lied to Winston and Julia in an effort to build up their hope for rebellion and trap them into arrest, torture, and deep psychological manipulation at the Ministry of Love.

Through the description of Hate Week and the extra hours Winston must spend at work due to the sudden change of enemies in the middle of the propaganda-filled week, we again see the degree to which the Party can successfully manipulate people's minds. The Party changes enemies in the middle of a speech from Eurasia to Eastasia, and immediately claims that Oceania has *always* been at war with Eastasia. Here, the phenomenon of doublethink is displayed clearly and powerfully. The masses accept this new enemy and the claim that Eastasia has always been the enemy with phenomenal ease.

Chapter IX consists almost entirely of excerpts from "the book," Goldstein's *The Theory and Practice of Oligarchical Collectivism.* When Julia arrives and finds Winston with the book, we again see the differences between them. Julia, more interested in her own personal survival than the future of the human race, is only vaguely interested, and after asking Winston to read aloud, falls asleep. Meanwhile, Winston is deeply fascinated by Goldstein's words and believes that the book will unlock the key to the mysteries behind the Party and its rule over Oceania. This section of the book reads largely like a history textbook, and provides a glimpse into Orwell's view of how Socialist revolutions have been abandoned by its champions to develop totalitarian regimes. We can assume that Orwell is drawing significantly from Stalin's rise to power and the institution of Stalinism in the Union of Soviet Socialist Republics. This section has often been criticized for an excess of academic analysis, but others cite it as supporting the novel's focus on the negative effects of totalitarian regimes. In this section, we can see how closely linked the world of *1984* is to historical events.

During this long discourse on global political developments, Julia is lulled to sleep and Winston eventually follows, but only after he realizes that the book has not told him anything new. Winston and Julia wake in the morning with a false sense of safety and serenity that is interrupted quite dramatically with the invasion of the Thought Police. Only moments earlier, Winston and Julia had again gazed down at the singing prole woman, and Winston had imagined a world filled with simple humanity. Yet it was during this hopeful moment that the Thought Police arrived. Winston has always known he would be arrested, but the scene is a dramatic surprise for the reader. The inevitable day has come.

# Summary and Analysis of Part Three I-III

Winston sits in a holding cell with white porcelain walls, no windows, and a high ceiling. He isn't sure where he is, but assumes that it is the Ministry of Love. The room is filled with light, and there is a low humming sound that Winston assumes is coming from the air system. A bench runs around the outside of the room, there is a telescreen on each of the four walls, and a lavatory pan sits in one corner. Winston is hungry, and has lost track of how long it has been since he has eaten, or even since he was arrested. Perhaps a day, perhaps two. He tries to sit as still as possible to avoid the wrath of the voices behind the telescreen, but after remembering he might have a piece of crust in his pocket, he succumbs to temptation. Immediately, the voice behind the telescreen yells, "Smith! 6079 Smith W.! Hands out of pockets in the cells!" Winston complies.

Before this cell, Winston was in another, far dirtier, cell, with at least ten to fifteen people in it at any given time. Most were proles or common criminals, and a few others were Party political prisoners. The common criminals were far less afraid. They fought against the prison guards, wrote on the walls, yelled back at the telescreen, and blatantly ate the food they had smuggled in, while the Party prisoners sat in terrified, obedient silence. Interestingly, the guards seemed to treat the common criminals more leniently. Winston gathered from what he heard in his cell that the work camps were "all right...so long as you had good contacts and knew the ropes," but the worst jobs in the forced labor camps were always given to political prisoners.

Winston observed the prisoners as they came and went. At one point, the guards brought in a very large woman, kicking and screaming, and unceremoniously dumped her across Winston's lap. She sat up, swore at the guards, and apologized to Winston by saying, "I wouldn't 'a sat on you, only the buggers put me there. They dono 'ow to treat a lady, do they?" Next, she vomited, and then, once recovered, put her arm around Winston and asked his name. Her last name was Smith as well, and she noted that is was even possible that she was his mother. Winston was struck by the possibility, but did not pursue the matter. None of the other prisoners spoke to Winston, but he overheard whispered, fearful conversations regarding Room 101.

In the white-walled cell, Winston thinks about what is going to happen to him. He imagines being beaten and tortured, and screaming for mercy. He rarely thinks of Julia, and finds it hard to fix her image in his mind. He wonders if O'Brien knows he has been arrested, and remembers him saying that even though the Brotherhood cannot ever help a prisoner, it might be able to smuggle him a razor blade. Winston hopes for the razor blade, imagining how quickly he might be able to end his life. Winston loses track of time completely, recognizing that with the lights always on, the Ministry of Love truly is "the place with no darkness." Suddenly, Ampleforth is thrown into the cell. He is dirty, shoeless, and clearly in a poor state. The two men talk, and Ampleforth says that he although he is not sure, he thinks he has been arrested because he left the word "God" in a Kipling poem. There was simply no other way to rhyme the couplet. They continue talking, but the telescreen quickly silences them. The guards return for Ampleforth, and he is sent to Room 101. Some time passes, and the guards return again, this time with Tom Parsons. Winston is shocked: he never expected Parsons to be arrested. Parsons is visibly upset, and begins asking Winston if they will shoot him. He expresses confidence that he will receive a fair trial, and hopes that his loyalty to the Party will keep his labor camp sentence short. Winston asks Parsons whether he is guilty, to which Parsons replies, "Of course I'm guilty! You don't think the Party would arrest an innocent man, do you?" He then tells Winston how his seven-year-old daughter listened at his bedroom door at night and heard him saying "Down with Big Brother!" in his sleep. He absolutely believes that he is guilty of saying it, and is proud of his daughter for doing her duty to the Party in reporting him. Parsons then uses the lavatory in a loud and obscene manner, smelling up the room for hours to come.

Parsons is eventually taken out, and other prisoners come and go. Some are relegated to Room 101, and Winston begins to notice that a few people tremble in great fear upon hearing those words. The guards bring in a man so emaciated that it seems he is being starved to death. One man offers him a piece of bread, but the telescreen quickly shouts him down, "2713 Bumstead J.! Let fall that piece of bread!" He does as he is told. Guards burst into the room, and Bumstead is punched so hard that he is sent flying across the room. Two halves of a dental plate fall out of his mouth, and blood gushes from his face. He pulls himself up to a sitting position, and Winston notices that his mouth is extremely swollen and bruised. All the other prisoners sit quietly. A guard opens the door and tells the starving man to go to Room 101. He immediately gasps and protests, his face turning a shade of green, begging for anything but Room 101, even telling the guard he would rather they cut his wife's and children's throats than take him there. In a panic, he looks around the room, finds Bumstead, the man who tried to give him a piece of bread, and argues that the guards should take him because he is a true enemy to the Party. Finally he throws himself to the ground, grabbing a leg of one of the benches and howling, begging not to go to Room 101. Ignoring his pleas, the guards struggle with him, break his hands free, and escort him from the room while all the other prisoners sit quietly and watch.

Many hours pass. Winston is desperately hungry and thirsty, and his thoughts of Julia and O'Brien wane. The doors open, and O'Brien walks in. Winston thinks O'Brien has also been captured, but O'Brien explains, "The got me a long time ago...You knew this Winston. Don't deceive yourself. You did know it - You have always known it." The guard with O'Brien hits Winston in the elbow, and he buckles in pain. The guard laughs, and Winston realizes that in the face of pain, there are no heroes. Nothing is worse than physical pain.

Winston wakes, and realizes that he is lying on a cot. O'Brien and a man with a hypodermic syringe are standing next to him. He does not know how long he has been unconscious, and has no concept of how long he has been undergoing torture. It might have been months, weeks, days, or only hours. He has been interrogated and forced to admit to a long list of crimes, and has been regularly and viciously beaten, suffering deep bruises and fractures all over his body. Sometimes, he knows, he screamed for mercy before anyone even hit him, and other times he convinced himself he would wait to confess until the pain became unbearable. After some time, the beatings became less frequent. When his questioners became Party intellectuals, he was forced to suffer face slapping, ear ringing, and standing on one foot for long periods of time. The complicated stream of questions could go on for hours, catching him in self-contradictions and leading him to a state of nervous fatigue. Sometimes they were nice to him, and spoke to him as though he were an equal, but then they would turn on him quickly. To gain their approval, he confessed to any and everything he could think of, including the assassination of Party members and various traitorous acts.

Throughout all of this, O'Brien is always nearby, guiding and defining the extent of Winston's torture. Winston finds himself strapped into a chair with O'Brien at his side, sitting next to a dial and a lever. O'Brien turns a lever, and Winston is overcome with pain. O'Brien continues talking to Winston, warning him that the dial goes all the way up to 100. He explains to Winston that he is taking the trouble to truly work with him to correct his mental derangement and defective memory. He begins by asking Winston what country Oceania is at war with, and what country Oceania has always been at war with. He then moves on to the newspaper clipping Winston found regarding Jones, Aaronson and Rutherford. He produces a copy of the photograph, places it in a memory hole, and explains that it never existed. He forces Winston to understand that the past does not exist in space, and therefore only exists in records and in human memory. In controlling these two things, the Party controls the past. Winston argues that the Party has not controlled his memory, and O'Brien counters that in fact, Winston has not controlled his own memory. He is at the Ministry of Love because he "failed in humanity, in self-discipline...would not make the act of submission which is the price of sanity." O'Brien explains, "Reality exists in the human mind, and nowhere else."

O'Brien begins forcing Winston to destroy this last vestige of his independent spirit. He works to show him that if the Party says that two plus two makes five, it does. Throughout this entire exchange, O'Brien tortures Winston with the dial, turning it up to 60, and perhaps beyond. Finally, O'Brien releases the dial and puts his arm around Winston. In his heart, Winston still has not admitted that two and two can actually make five. O'Brien begins again, the needle travels higher, and Winston becomes increasingly desperate. O'Brien reveals to Winston that people are brought to the Ministry of Love not to force them to confess, but to cure them. He discusses how past regimes tortured and killed their enemies, but did not work to change them. In contrast, the Party converts and changes their enemies, making them "one of their own" before killing them. He tells Winston, "We will crush you down to the point from which there is no coming back...Never again will you be capable of ordinary human feeling...friendship, or joy of living...courage or integrity."

O'Brien orders a new form of punishment similar to electroshock therapy while continuing his line of questioning. Finally, he is successful in convincing Winston that his memory is flawed. At the end of the session, when Winston is almost able to actually see five fingers where there are only four, O'Brien reveals that he likes Winston, because his mind reminds him of his own, except that Winston's mind is deranged. He then allows Winston to ask him questions, and Winston asks about Julia. She has betrayed him, and every part of her independence has been destroyed. Winston asks if Big Brother exists. O'Brien answers that he does, in the way that the Party does, but that he will never die. Winston asks if the Brotherhood exists, and O'Brien says that Winston will never know the answer to that question. Winston asks what is in Room 101. O'Brien answers, "You know what is in Room 101, Winston. Everyone knows what is in Room 101."

Winston is again tied down, flat on his back. O'Brien mentions Winston's diary entry, in which he wrote "I understand how; I do not understand why." In reference to this, O'Brien mentions Goldstein's book and reveals that he collaborated in writing it. Winston asks if it is accurate, and O'Brien replies that the book's notion of enlightenment and proletarian rebellion is nonsense. The Party can never be overthrown: "The Party is forever." After explaining this fact, O'Brien asks Winston why the Party exists. Knowing the correct answer, but not believing it, Winston replies, "You are ruling over us for our own good." O'Brien turns the dial, and explains to Winston that the Party "seeks power entirely for its own sake...We are not interested in the good of others; we are interested solely in power." He compares the Party to the German Nazis and Russian Communists, but argues that the Party is far superior because it has no illusions of equality. The Party embraces power for the sake of power, not for any other cause. In utter submission, individuals can become part of a greater, immortal whole: the Party. As such, "Freedom is Slavery...[and] Slavery is Freedom." O'Brien continues, explaining that the Party defines all, including the laws of nature, and explains that before man, there was no world. Without human consciousness, nothing exists. Winston argues that dinosaurs and ancient beasts lives before humans, and O'Brien counters that 19th-century scientists made those stories up. Man is the center of the universe, the earth is the center of the universe: "Outside man there is nothing."

O'Brien pauses this philosophical discussion to return to the main issue of power over man, which is achieved through making men suffer. Progress will work towards more pain, more hatred, and more destruction. Art, science and literature will disappear. There will be no way to distinguish beauty from ugliness. O'Brien describes "a world of victory, triumph after triumph after triumph: an endless pressing, pressing, pressing on the nerve of power." Winston disagrees, claiming that such a society would die of its own accord. He tells O'Brien that the Party will never overcome "the spirit of Man." O'Brien counters that if Winston is a man, he is the last one on earth. Winston admits feeling superior to O'Brien, at which point O'Brien plays a tape revealing the irony of Winston's statement in which Winston agrees to do anything in support of the Brotherhood, including murder, espionage, etc.

O'Brien forces Winston to look at his naked body in a mirror. Winston is horrified to see his gray, weak, bowed body. He is emaciated, has gone partially bald, is extremely dirty, and carries innumerable scars. He can barely recognize himself. O'Brien ridicules his appearance, showing him how he is rotting away, and even pulling out one of his remaining teeth. Winston breaks down, and O'Brien assures him that he can escape from this hell if he so chooses. Winston refuses to accept defeat, claiming that he still has not betrayed his love for Julia. Winston asks when he will be shot, and O'Brien says it might be a long time, but that in the end, it will happen.

Analysis

Part Two describes both the beginning and the end of Winston and Julia's affair. Their arrest separates them for the entirety of their time at the Ministry of Love. In this way, Winston's only true act of rebellion is over. Winston's torture proves to be as horrific as he always imagined. He easily concludes that physical pain is the worst thing in the world, and entirely unbearable. During the process of torture, O'Brien quickly gains control over him and begins to penetrate his mind through deep psychological manipulation, assisted by electroshock therapy. In the hands of O'Brien and the Ministry of Love, Winston cannot stop the process of his psychological and physical destruction.

O'Brien is a pivotal character throughout this section, and it is here that we finally gain insight into his thus far mysterious mind. He is an ardent Party supporter and believes deeply in the purity of his mission and work. Interestingly, Winston's fatalistic outlook continues in prison, as he acknowledges that somewhere deep down, he probably knew all along that O'Brien was a Party supporter. In truth, Winston knew he would be arrested before he met with O'Brien, and therefore the meeting neither increased nor decreased his risk. Perhaps Winston did imagine O'Brien was a Party supporter, but wanted to trust him and believe in the Brotherhood so badly that he disregarded these thoughts. Winston's dream, seven years ago, of O'Brien's voice telling him they would "meet in the place where there is no darkness" led Winston to obsess over O'Brien and gave him hope that he might be a source of support. O'Brien becomes Winston's hero; even in his torture sessions he is calmer when O'Brien is near. As O'Brien points out, Winston once wrote in his diary that it did not matter whether O'Brien was on his side or not, because he felt the man understood him. Ironically, Winston seems to love O'Brien, even throughout the torture process, and as such comes to believe the Party propaganda he has so long rebelled against.

In this section, Winston finally gets an answer to his question, "Why?" O'Brien reveals to him that the Party pursues power for the sake of power, and for no other goal. This is why the Party is able to define the present, the past, and every facet of society. Here, we also see how the Party has broken from Socialism and the Revolution to embrace totalitarian rule. This is Orwell's greatest frustration with totalitarian regimes. Orwell watched as supposedly Socialist revolutions broke down into totalitarian regimes, specifically in the case of the Stalinist Union of Soviet Socialist Republics and Hitler's Nazi Germany. These regimes spoke of their goal of improving life for the common man, yet in actuality simply sought power. In *1984*, the Party admits to its goal of power for power's sake. This totalitarian society, efficient in quelling all dissent and individuality, and in defining itself and the world, is the ultimate dystopia.

Winston's torture process reveals the degree of violence prisoners are subjected to. They are starved, beaten, and deformed; brought to their weakest point, and then finally given salvation. When wholly broken, the prisoner's spirit and mind will finally give in to manipulation. Winston is almost physically destroyed in the process of his torture, but only after he *sees* the shell he has become does he submit to O'Brien. O'Brien becomes his savior in the next chapters, allowing him to eat, heal and grow strong. As his savior, O'Brien greatly influences Winston's mind and thought processes, guiding him to the ways of the Party and removing all sense of individuality and independence.

# Summary and Analysis of Part Three IV-VI

Winston is still in the Ministry of Love, but his health is steadily improving. He is eating well and continually growing stronger. He has been given a pillow and a mattress for his wooden bed, has had a bath, and has been permitted to wash himself in a small basin. He also has new underclothes and clean overalls. Winston is unsure of the exact timeframe, but thinks that weeks or months have gone by. He has been dreaming a great deal, largely of the Golden Country, his mother, Julia, and O'Brien. He is happy and peaceful in his dreams. Eventually, he begins to exercise, walking around the cell and experimenting with carrying and lifting weight. When he is able to complete a pushup, he feels a great sense of accomplishment. Soon, he begins to use the slate and pencil he has been given. Working through what he and O'Brien discussed, Winston analyzes his perspective of the world. He realizes that he cannot fight against the Party, and that O'Brien is correct in stating that sanity is statistical. He writes on his slate, "Freedom is Slavery, Two and Two Make Five." Then he hesitates, forgetting what comes next, reasons it out, and writes "God is Power." He accepts that the past is alterable, he accepts the Party's rule, and he accepts that he has been wrong. He thinks, "Only surrender, and everything else followed."

Winston sleeps, and in his dream calls out Julia's name. He wakes himself with this exclamation and immediately realizes that he has set himself back significantly by revealing this weakness. He had surrendered his mind, but not his heart. As he expects, Winston hears boots walking up to his door. O'Brien enters and tells Winston to follow him. O'Brien explains that intellectually, there is little wrong with Winston, but emotionally, he has made no progress. Demanding honesty, O'Brien asks Winston what he thinks of Big Brother. Winston replies, "I hate him." O'Brien notes that the time has come for Winston to love Big Brother. He sends Winston to Room 101.

O'Brien meets him in Room 101, and explains to Winston that Room 101 is "the worst thing in the world," which is different for each individual. For Winston, the worst thing in the world is rats. Winston sees the cage and begins to scream protests. O'Brien picks up the cage, which houses huge rats, and sets it down next to Winston. O'Brien explains that rats are carnivorous, and are known to eat infants and attack sick or dying people. The cage has a mask that will fit over Winston's head. A lever release will force the cage door up, allowing the rats access to Winston's face. They will attack him, gouging his eye, cheeks, and tongue. Winston is in a panic. He realizes that he must put someone else between himself and the horror of the cage. He feels "blind, helpless, mindless" in his fear. When the mask is inches from his face, he screams, "Do it to Julia!" He begs O'Brien to force Julia to suffer in his place. O'Brien is satisfied.

Winston has been released from the Ministry of Love. He sits in the Chestnut Tree Cafe drinking their special clove-flavored Victory Gin. Winston listens to the telescreen, eager for a special bulletin from the Ministry of Peace. There should be news about Central Africa. Suddenly, his mind wanders. He has trouble focusing on any single thought these days. He can smell the gin, and thinks of how it is forever mixed up with the smell of the rats he faced, although he never names the beasts. A waiter who recognizes Winston as a regular brings him a chessboard and a *Times* before filling his gin glass. He begins to examine the chess problem in the *Times*: "White to play and mate in two moves." He looks at Big Brother, thinking to himself, "White always mates."

The telescreen announces that a bulletin will be given at fifteen-thirty. He is excited to think of the news. Eurasia is invading Central Africa, and if they are successful may eventually succeed in splitting Oceania in two, which could mean the destruction of the Party. Unconsciously, he traces "2+2=5" in the dust on the table, and thinks of Julia. They saw each other once after being released, purely by chance. He followed her on her walk, always a few feet behind. Eventually she stopped and he put his arm around her waist, but felt revulsion at the thought of making love to her. She did not respond; her body felt rigid and lifeless. They sat down on a bench with some distance between them. After some time, she told him, "I betrayed you." He told her the same. They agreed, through a distant conversation, that there are some things they can do to you that make you think and care only about yourself. After that, it is impossible to ever feel the same way towards one who you loved. She made an excuse to leave, and they both feebly suggested they should meet again, knowing they never would. Winston followed her for a short time, but eventually lost her in a crowd and gave up the effort.

Sitting in the Chestnut Tree Cafe, Winston feels nostalgic, and tears up when the song "Under the spreading Chestnut Tree, I sold you and you sold me" begins to play over the telescreen. The waiter brings him more gin. Winston reflects on how his life is now filled with gin. It is "his life, his death, and his resurrection." Winston is a fixture at the Chestnut Tree Cafe, despite his new position as a sinecure, meaning he is on a sub-committee under many other sub-committees, and only goes to work a couple of days out of the week. He does little, but is paid well. Winston's thoughts turn back to the battle in Africa. He wonders if there even is a battle. Suddenly, a strong memory comes to him. Winston was nine or ten, sitting on the floor and shaking a dice box, laughing with excitement. His mother was sitting across from him, and also laughing. It was a brief moment, in their hard lives, of happiness and camaraderie. His mother had gone out in the rain to buy him the board game as a reward for behaving well. For a whole afternoon, Winston, his mother, and his sister had a wonderful, joyous time.

Winston pushes the memory out of his mind, certain that it is one of those false memories that keeps troubling him. Suddenly, a loud trumpet call sounds, signaling that the bulletin is about to be announced. Oceania has intelligently outflanked Eurasia, capturing the whole of Africa and perhaps bringing the war close to an end. It is the greatest victory in history. Winston listens to the news with excitement, thinking it has all turned out just as he had thought it would. His feet stir beneath him, and he imagines himself running with the cheering crowds out in the street. He looks at the poster of Big Brother and is in awe of his greatness. He recognizes that only ten minutes ago he had wondered if Oceania might be defeated. But now, staring into the warm, strong eyes of Big Brother, he realizes that this could never be. With tears of great understanding trickling down his face, Winston realizes he has finally defeated himself. He loves Big Brother.

Analysis

These chapters describe Winston's recovery from his near-death experience in the Ministry of Love. O'Brien continues to be his savior, allowing Winston to heal, benefit from basic comforts such as a mattress and a pillow, and gain back his strength. In this process, Winston begins to fully accept O'Brien's version of the world. Without the Party, there is nothing. Here, we see the effectiveness of the combination of O'Brien's physical and psychological torture. Winston, a lone man, has no hope for successfully rebuffing these invasions into his body and mind. He is overcome through force and power. Knowing he has been beaten, Winston still wonders when he will be finally be killed, when the Party will finally decide his life is over.

Winston reveals that his conversion is incomplete when he yells out Julia's name in his sleep. O'Brien methodically observes Winston's behavior, waiting to see exactly how much progress he has made. When Winston calls out in his sleep, O'Brien knows there is still some vestige of individual thought left in Winston's mind. He loves Julia, and to be a successful Party member, he can only have love for Big Brother. To remedy this dysfunction, O'Brien brings Winston to Room 101. The rat cage stretches Winston's sanity to its breaking point. To some, the rat cage might seem a simple tool, not threatening enough to demand Winston's final submission. However, we previously learned that Winston's greatest fear was rats. This fear is innate, and lies deep in his subconscious. Therefore, presenting him with the danger of sitting fully conscious in a chair and having his face eaten by rats is the worst possible threat Winston can face. In this scene, Orwell argues yet again that physical pain is the worst thing a person can face. Winston is unable to fight against the potential horror of rats eating his face, and submits almost immediately. In this pivotal scene, Winston loses all hope of maintaining his individual spirit or his love for Julia. They once promised each other that the Party could never take away their love for each other, but now they have been proven wrong.

Although his love for Julia is removed, as we see through the failure of their accidental meeting, Winston does not yet love Big Brother. Back in Oceanian society, Winston is a shell of a man. The totalitarian regime has broken him. The reader might once have seen Winston as hope for a brighter future for Oceania, and for the end of Party rule. Here, in the final chapters, we come to understand that there is no hope for rebellion against such a regime. The Party's power is total, and once that power is obtained, there is no way to reverse it. In the last scene, Winston finally comes to love Big Brother, and in so doing notes that he has finally beaten himself.

The man as we first knew him has ceased to exist. Winston has submitted to complete psychological control by the Party.

In reflecting on this conclusion, it is important to note that Winston was one of few members of Oceanian society who even remembered a time before the Revolution. Julia, although disgruntled with Party life, never believed in the potential for successful rebellion. It is easy to assume that once the last people who remember life before the Revolution die off, and once Newspeak officially takes over for Oldspeak, thus removing the citizens' ability to even *think* against the Party, there will be no hope for Winston's ideals. The Party's control will be absolute, and it is difficult to see any scenario that would break it. Here, we have Orwell's final warning. He suggests that allowing totalitarian regimes to develop and take hold is the equivalent of placing society on a path towards violent governance and absolute removal of individual thoughts and freedoms; in other words, towards the ultimate dystopia.

# Suggested Essay Questions

1. Compare and contrast Julia and Winston. How does each rebel against the Party, and are these rebellions at all effective?
2. Trace Winston's path towards destruction. Where do we first see his fatalistic outlook? Is his defeat inevitable?
3. Discuss the role of technology in Oceania. In what areas is technology highly advanced, and in what areas has its progress stalled? Why?
4. Discuss the role of Big Brother in Oceania and in Winston's life. What role does Big Brother play in each?
5. Discuss contradiction in Oceania and the Party's governance, i.e. Ministry of Love, Ministry of Truth, Ministry of Plenty, Ministry of Peace. Why is such contradiction accepted so widely?
6. Discuss and analyze the role O'Brien plays in Winston's life. Why is he such a revered and respected character, even during Winston's time in the Ministry of Love?
7. Discuss the symbolic importance of the prole woman singing in the yard behind Mr. Charrington's apartment. What does she represent for Winston, and what does she represent for Julia?
8. 1984 is a presentation of Orwell's definition of dystopia and was meant as a warning to those of the modern era. What specifically is Orwell warning us against, and how does he achieve this?
9. Analyze the interactions between Winston and the old man in the pub, Syme, and Mr. Charrington. How do Winston's interactions with these individuals guide him towards his ultimate arrest?
10. Analyze the Party's level of power over its citizens, specifically through the lens of psychological manipulation. Name the tools the Party uses to maintain this control and discuss their effectiveness.
11. Outline the social hierarchy of Oceania. How does this hierarchy support the Party and its goals?

# Newspeak

The book's Appendix provides a detailed discussion of Newspeak, the official language of Oceania. Interestingly, the Appendix is written in the past tense, as though a historian is examining a past culture. Some argue that this tool suggests that the Party eventually falls.

The Appendix details the underlying principles of Newspeak. Essentially, the language was designed to limit the range of thought. The word classes are detailed as follows:

The A vocabulary consisted of everyday words used in the expression of simple thoughts, usually involving concrete objects or physical actions.

The B vocabulary consisted of words created to hold political connotations and impose a politically desirable state of mind upon the user. Such words include compound words, like "Ingsoc" or "doublethink." Many meant the opposite of what they really were, in keeping with the concept of doublethink.

The C vocabulary consisted of scientific and technical terms, which behooved no one but scientists and technicians to use.

The grammar of Newspeak had two notable characteristics. First, there was an almost complete interchangeability between different parts of speech. A noun and a verb were basically the same, and formed the root for all other forms of the word. Adjectives were formed by tacking "-ful" onto the end of the word, i.e. "goodthinkful"; adverbs, by adding the suffix "-wise." Any word could be negated by the prefix "un-," and other prefixes like "plus-" and "doubleplus-" could strengthen the word, i.e "pluscold" and "doublepluscold." Second, the grammar was exceedingly regular, with very few exceptions. All past tenses were formed using "-ed," all plurals with "-s" or "-es," and comparatives with "-er" and "-est."

Euphony was privileged above everything except precision of meaning, because the end goal was to produce words that could be spoken so quickly that they would not have the time to prompt thought. In other words, people would be able to speak without thinking at all. The meanings of Newspeak words were carefully controlled so that in many cases most connotations were destroyed. For instance, the word "free" still existed, but only in the sense of something being "free from" something else, e.g. "This field is free from weeds." It could not be used with reference to political freedom, as this meaning had been drilled out of the word.

Newspeak therefore also precluded the ability to argue heretical opinions. Although it would have been possible to say "Big Brother is ungood," the words necessary to defend or argue this assertion did not exist. Through this process, Oldspeak (standard English) would become obsolete and impossible to understand or translate, since the meanings of its words would be impossible to express in Newspeak. As Winston's friend Syme states, in explaining how Newspeak will support the Party's goals, "Orthodoxy means not thinking - not needing to think. Orthodoxy is unconsciousness."

Some Newspeak words highlighted in the text include:

Ingsoc - English Socialism

Doublethink - The ability to simultaneously think two opposing thoughts.

Thoughtcrime - Anti-Party thoughts

Facecrime - Occurs when the face reveals the existence of thoughtcrime (either lacking in anti-Party vigor, or expressing distaste for Party actions).

Goodthinkful - Describes a person who thinks just as the Party wishes. Winston describes Katharine this way.

Speakwrite - A machine that transposes spoken word into written word.

Unperson - Someone the Party has vaporized; someone that no longer exists.

Doubleplusungood - Extremely bad.

# Author of ClassicNote and Sources

Christina Shelby, author of ClassicNote. Completed on July 30, 2007, copyright held by GradeSaver.

Updated and revised Jordan Berkow September 19, 2007. Copyright held by GradeSaver.

Orwell, George. 1984. New York: Signet Classic, 1949.

Crick, Bernard. George Orwell: A Life. Boston: Little, Brown, 1980.

Steinhoff, William R. George Orwell and the Origins of 1984. Ann Arbor: University of Michigan Press, 1975.

Howe, Irving. 1984 Revisited: Totalitarianism in Our Century. New York: Harper Row, 1983.

Hitchens, Christopher. Why Orwell Matters. New York: Basic Books, 2003.

Cushman, Thomas, and Rodden, John. George Orwell: Into the Twenty-First Century. Boulder: Paradigm Publishers, 2004.

# Essay: The Reflection of George Orwell

**by Crystal Epps**
**August 23, 2000**

> "On each landing, opposite the lift shaft, the poster with the enormous face gazed from the wall. It was one of those pictures which are so contrived that the eyes follow you about when you move. BIG BROTHER IS WATCHING YOU, the caption beneath it ran." (Orwell 4 "Nineteen").

George Orwell's Nineteen Eighty-Four presents a negative utopian picture, a society ruled by rigid totalitarianism. The government which Orwell creates in his novel is ruled by an entity known as Big Brother and consists of four branches. The Ministry of Truth, overseeing the distribution of propaganda and other printed materials, the Ministry of Peace (dealing with war), the Ministry of Plenty, handling economic affairs, and the Ministry of Love, the law enforcement division, make up the government. The main character, Winston Smith, does not completely accept the ideology that is fed to him by the government, through the concept of Big Brother. When one examines George Orwell's life, it can be clearly seen that he personifies his political perceptions, social and aesthetic characteristics, and self-examination of his own writing, through Winston Smith, in Nineteen Eighty-Four.

Orwell's political perceptions, especially his skepticism of mass media, are given life through Winston Smith. Spending time working for the British Broadcasting Company (BBC), Orwell experienced many distorted truths and propaganda (Woodcock 9). This led to an intense distrust of those in power and their influence on the information distributed to and recieved by the general public. Orwell explains how history is altered by whomever is in power. In Orwell's essay "Revising History" he examines the credibility of history and finds that it is based on the person or group in control. Orwell hated totalitarianism, primarily because of its attacks on unbiased truth and so saw it as the enemy. If a person or organization in power finds a fact damaging or out of sync with his cause, he can simply change it by the manner in which it is reported. Orwell states, "A certain degree of truthfulness was possible so long as it was admitted that a fact may be true even if you don't like it." ("Revising" 1). He is supporting his ideas with an obvious example familiar to most. World War II, Orwell points out, had two very distinct slants depending on whether you subscribe to the Nazi account or that of their enemies. Another telling example he spoke of was the broadcasted outcome of the Spanish Civil War being decided by the winning power's preferences. Simply put, Orwell boldly claims that "History is written by the winners," (Orwell, "Revising" 1). So Orwell's own distrust is obvious in his creation of the Ministry of Truth. It is here where his main character, Winston, is employed forming propaganda and changing past facts to coincide with whatever lies Big Brother is feeding the general public. According to Woodcock, Orwell definitely based the Ministry of Truth and Winston's work on his experiences at the

BBC (9). Winston's role in Big Brother's government was a projected chariceristic of Orwell's political opinions.

Furter exemplifying the attribution of Orwell's characteristics through Winston Smith, is the manifestation of Orwell's political views in Winston's own writings. Although Orwell wrote publicly, and Winston wrote in a private diary, they both passionately wrote for their own cause. Orwell was against totalitarianism and used Winston to reflect that when he wrote against the "evils of Igsoc" (Duda 1). Igsoc is the doctirne by which the government of Oceania, under which Winston lived, was operated. In Nineteen Eighty-Four, Winston Smith writes in his diary: "For whom, it suddenly occurred to him to wonder was he writing this diary? For the future, for the unborn . . ." "For the first time the magnitude of what he had undertaken came home to him. How could you communicate with the future? It was of its nature impossible. Either the future would resemble the present in which case it would not listen to him, or it would be different from it, and his predicament would be meaningless" (10). Although both Winston and Orwell recognize their objective is hopeless, they still cling to the hope that maybe through their words and descriptions, (as opposed to logical arguments) that they might, even for a moment alter another's thinking (Duda 2). Orwell writes in his essay, "Why I Write" that "Every line of serious work that I have written since 1936 has been written directly or indirectly against totalitarianism and for democratic socialism, as I understand it" (4). Serving as England's "moral conscience," he sought to boldly reveal the truth, even to those who denied its existence (Kollar 2). Winston, much like Orwell, seemed to be sole possesor of any sort of a sense of morality as he struggled against immense odds to reveal the inequity and unjust nature of the government. Winston and Orwell both had overcome the problem of communication to others; in order to be understood, the person receiving the message must have similar a "world-view" (Duda 1). Winston writes in his diary, "Until they become conscious they will never rebel, and until after they have rebelled they cannot become conscious" (Orwell, "Nineteen" 61) Winston, trying to overcome the oppression by Big Brother and Orwell is writing to those oppressed by Communism and cannot be reached by Western publications and are oblivious to his work. He recognizes that one "Can only preach to the converted" (Duda 1).Writing not to create some wonderful, entertaining work, instead, Orwell,s motive was to reveal lies, expose them to the public, and make his views known (Orwell, "Why" 4). In "Why I Write" Orwell explains one of his primary reasons for writing as a "political purpose", a desire to alter other's political direction, to change the world (2). Orwell sought to have a purpose in life, much like Winston. A monotonous lifestyle was not enough for Winston, who felt the need to somehow be influential. As a result he became obsessed with politics and his rebellion against totaitariansim. Everything Winston does has political motives, even sex (Magill 1553). Orwell's political motives behind his writing, and his goal to expose the truth to the public was demonstrated repeatedly through Winston Smith's character.

Yet another example of a revelation of Orwell's character through Winstons is the similarly displayed attitudes towards authority figures and upper level government officials. According to Grigson, Nineteen Eighty-Four is not so much about a Utopia as it is "power and corruption at high levels" (343). Woodcock explains that Orwell was, in his novel, expressing his concerns about men in power who would sacrifice everything for a mere crumb of power (343). O'Brien, an inner party member and Winston's boss, brags of the Party's "eternal power" much like Hitler boasted of the" millennial Reich", a leader viewed warily by Orwell (Woodcock 219). Winston is unsure of his relationship with O'Brien, whether he is freind or foe, and his opinions of him fluctuate throughout the book. However, despite his hate of dictators, Orwell felt a certain, unexplainable, sympathy for Hitler, much like Winston, who at the end of Nineteen Eighty-Four realizes that he loves Big Brother (Woodcock 57). Again, Orwell has created Winston to hold his own perceptions of governmental leaders, thus holding the image of Orwell's political beliefs.

In addition, Orwell displays his understanding of social economic classes through Winston. In Nineteen Eighty-Four, Winston often takes long walks among the Prole section, finding comfort in their masses. Visiting the Chestnut Tree Cafe, Winston takes advantage of the absence of a telescreen which is normally present everywhere, monitoring every move, to speak to an old man about the past. Winston loves the objects of the Proles, and when he finds a glass ornament with a piece of coral inside an antique shop, he buys it even though it is illegal to posess such objects. Renting a small apartment above the shop, he and Julia, his secret and illegal lover, go there often, as there is no telescreen. He enjoys just simply lounging, listening to the sounds of the lowest class. Like his main character, Orwell too found great comfort in the lower class. After serving 5 years in the Indian Imperial Police in Burma, Orwell realized that the oppression of the Burmese by the British was wrong and he could participate no more(Kollar 2). He left the comforts of middle class society in which one man places himself above another to live amongst the lowest classes of society. Orwell looked upon the lower class as "victims of injustice", and preferred them to his peers, the middle class, who ate unappreciatively off the plate that was prepared by the lower class (Kollar 2). Both Orwell and Winston loved to move about the poverty stricken lower classes. Feeling empathy and compassion towards them, Winston and Orwell were inspired, as they placed their trust for the future in the working class. Winston Smith's identification and preference toward the lower class was a direct result of Orwell's own social nature as a part of his personality.

Furthermore, Orwell continued to project his individuality in Winston in some very basic and ordinary manners. Winston has a relatively decent job as an Outer Party member in the Ministry of Truth. However, due to rations resulting from ceaseless wars, Winston is accustomed to scrimping and making the most of whatever he could buy. This stems from Orwell's life as a writer where, during the writing of a book, he practiced frugality until income was received for a publishing. Winston, as an Outer Party member, is not part of the elite Inner Party but neither is he in the lowest class, known as the Proles. Orwell was also middle class. Orwell was said to lack close friends with whom he could discuss deep issues and share his problems (Coppard, Crick 15). Winston also lacked someone with whom to share his deepest feelings. Although Winston had Julia, she did not care to discuss any kind of politics, instead their relationship was much more superficial. Both being unattractive, Orwell often complained of being ugly and had a lot of health problems, just like Winston who is described as being small and frail with a course face (Coppard, Crick 53). Sharing Orwell's negative attitude, Winston describes much in the novel as "looking like vomit" (Magill 1532). Winston can be obviously seen as a direct personification of George Orwell.

Examining yet again his motives behind writing, Orwell used Winston Smith to explain a basic need he felt simply to record history. In Orwell's essay, "Why I Write", he describes writing as a "historical impulse-- a desire to see things as they are, find out true facts and store them for use of posterity" (Orwell 2). In this passage from Nineteen Eighty-Four, Winston Smith is writing in a diary he bought: "For whom, it suddenly occurred to him to wonder was he writing this diary? For the future, for the unborn" (10). Duda explains how, in this passage, Winston is trying to deal with his intellectual rebellion by writing his thoughts in a diary, which is illegal and makes death inevitable. He recognizes that it will probably not have an effect, only quicken his death, but he still clings to the notion that some day it might be found and used to prove the nature of his present state (1). Winston is writing simply to record a piece of history, that it might be used by the future, another example of Orwell's influence on Winston's character, specifically his motivation for writing.

Orwell expressed many of his fears and self-doubts as a writer through the character Winston Smith. In describing Winston's writing, he is examining his own purposes in writing. For Orwell, writing is a means of bringing others to the thought. His basis of success is reliant on his effectiveness of reaching others (Duda 1). Orwell felt that his works without "political purpose" resulted in "lifeless books" and "sentences without meaning" (Orwell, "Why" 5). Feeling lonely and unappreciated as a child, Orwell knew that he was skilled with words, and felt that it somehow made up for some of his other weaknesses and failures (1). However, he was still very critical of himself, saying in reference to a book he was preparing to write: 'It is bound to be a failure, every book is a failure" (Orwell, "Why" 4). Smith's uncertainty of the worthwhileness of his writings is a direct reflection of Orwell's own wonderment of worth as a writer (Duda 1).

In the novel Nineteen Eighty-Four, Winston Smith is a direct personification of the author, George Orwell. This was seen through Orwell's political perceptions, such as his skepticism about mass media, his politically motivated writings, and his view of governmental figures. The characterization was also displayed in Orwell's attraction to a certain social, economic class, and his basic aesthetic similarities. Orwell's feelings about writing were also exhibited through Winston Smith; his fears of failure and his basic yearning to be remembered. Nineteen Eighty-Four will forever be remembered for its prophetic warnings of a totalitarian society in which individuality is stripped away. In a desperate attempt to pierce through invincible, omnipitant, omni-present Big Brother, Winston Smith fought to preserve his identity, an identity which was a true reflection of George Orwell.

**Works Cited**

Coppard, Audrey, and Bernard Crick. Orwell Remembered. New York, NY: Facts on File Publications. 1984: 15, 53.

Duda, John. "Orwell." 2 pgs. Online. America Online. 18 Jan. 1999. Available: http://dept.english.upenn.edu/~mstrong/dudaorwell.html.

Grigson, Geoffrey, ed. The Consice Encyclopedia of Modern World Literature. New York: Hawthorn Books Inc. 1963: 343.

Kollar, Maros. "George Orwell Biography." 4 pgs. Online. America Online. 18 Jan. 1999. Available: www.suldal.vgs.no/engelsk/orwell/bioorw.htm.

Magill, Frank N. ed. Survey of Science Fiction Literature. Vol. 3. Englewood Cliffs: Salem Press, 1979: 1532-1533.

Orwell, George."Revising History." As I Please 4 Feb. 1944. Online. America Online. 2 Jan. 1999: 1-2.

---.Nineteen Eighty-Four. Ontario: Penguin Books, 1949: 10, 61.

---."Why I Write." 1947: 5pgs. Online. America Online. 2 Jan. 1999. Available: www.resort.com/~prime8/orwell/whywrite.html.

Reilly, Patrick. Nineteen Eighty-Four: Past, Present and Future. Boston, MA: Twayne Publishers. 1989: xv, xvi.

Woodcock, George. The Crystal Spirit. Boston: Little, Brown and Company. 1966: 9, 57, 219, 258.

# Essay: Totalitarian Collectivism in 1984, or, Big Brother Loves You

**by Tiffany Shropshire**
**September 11, 2001**

Following the political upheaval and struggle for power after the second world war, George Orwell's novel 1984 cautions against the dangers of oppression and exemplifies the consequential nightmarish world of the near future. The plot traces the struggles of the main character, Winston Smith, as he attempts to rebel against the tyrannically insatiable Party, rulers of the superstate Oceania. In this terrifying glimpse of the future, independent thought, along with all other human values and ideals, is eradicated, and therein replaced only with fanatical loyalty to the Party and "unconscious orthodoxy." The Party, also known as Ingsoc, is able to achieve these ends with a complex utilization of manipulation mechanisms, eliminating free thought through the restrictive language, constant propaganda, degradation of human values, enforced social hierarchy, and virtual complete control of reality. The novel 1984 epitomizes, if not exaggerates, the horrors of a totalitarian collectivism, where a government can claim that a contradiction, such as two and two makes five, is true, and the hive mind will believe it.

The concept of language as a confining tool is an exceptionally important message of the book, and this is used to its full potential in the official language of Oceania, Newspeak. Language, of course, is of primary significance to the human thought process, and can be used to expand upon an individual's expression or severely limit it. In 1984, Ingsoc has mastered the theory behind communication with Newspeak, "the only language in the world whose vocabulary gets smaller every year." Basically, Newspeak is a way to narrow the range of thought until "a heretical thought (is) literally unthinkable, at least so far as thought is dependent on words." Thoughtcrime, or unorthodox thoughts, would become obsolete, because with no mode to express them, they could not exist. The Party constantly updates Newspeak and the Newspeak dictionary to forward their utmost intent that eventually no one will even be able to conceptualize questioning the Party's absolute authority.

Doublethink, the infamous Newspeak word for "reality control," is in itself an example of government oppression, where reality exists how the Party says it exists and nothing more. To be more accurate, the definition of double think would be "the power of holding two contradictory thoughts in one's mind simultaneously, and accepting both of them." This is integral to maintaining the idea that the Party is infallible and Big Brother is semi-divine. Doublethink is the neglection of all logic; if the Party says 'two and two make five,' it is a crime to think otherwise; the Party "could reach (the stars) if (they) wanted to...or (they) could blot them out." Altering history is not impossible, and falsifying records is in order, as "he who controls the past controls the present; who controls the present controls the future." Put simply, doublethink is controlled insanity.

Tremendous amounts of propaganda perpetuate the insanity, from the "ruggedly handsome" yet stern features of Big Brother, glaring from posters plastered on every wall and street corner, to the Hate-themed celebrations which excite crazed emotions from every citizen. Big Brother is substituted for God in an atheist society, that is, "B.B." is the source of all goodness and righteousness, and the target of all praise, whether in actual existence or not. All emotions suppressed by the Party are given only this outlet for expression; an overwhelming, devoted love to the Party and Big Brother, and a deep-rooted hatred for the "mortal enemy" of Oceania, or more accurately, the scapegoat. Even Winston, who throughout the novel attempts to reject Ingsoc's brainwashing, is swept away with the raw emotional flood of the Two Minute Hate; "it was impossible to avoid joining in...a hideous ecstasy of fear and vindictiveness, a desire to kill...turn(ed) one even against one's will into a grimacing, screaming lunatic." In 1984, propaganda is a constant flow of psychological stimuli, beginning at a very young age with the Junior Spies, through adolescence with the Junior Anti-Sex League, and continuing into adulthood under the permanent surveillance of the telescreens, barking out orders and information twenty-four hours a day. This early ingrainment in propaganda results in pent-up emotions released as the Party, and no one else, sees fit.

For the Party, the thirst for pure power, the means to its own end, causes the state of never-ending war with the other two superstates. The purpose of the war is two fold: first, war makes certain that all surplus supplies are wasted, and second, war provides a certain "wartime mentality" which keeps the people of Oceania obedient and in check. In turn, destroying supplies results in the class system, an important way to be sure that the one group in power, the High group of the Party, remains in power. In this way, the High strata reserves the best goods for themselves, the Middle receives the High's leftovers, and the Low is left to barely eke out an existence. With the Low, or the proles, constantly occupied with survival, they will always be apathetic towards politics, revolution, or government, because nothing takes more precedence than living for another day with food in the belly. The Party and the governments of the other superstates in the world realize this, and so unofficially agree to remain at constant war, in order to keep their place in power. To look at it one way, "in principle it would be quite simple to waste the surplus labor of the world...by producing vast quantities of goods and then setting fire to them...but this would provide only the economic and not the emotional basis for a hierarchical society." The emotional basis is that of the wartime mentality; when at war, the natural inclination is to support the country and support the government running it, basically handing over the country to be run as seen fit by the higher order who should know what they are doing. By maintaining the constant state of warfare, the Party is also able to control the lower classes from ever rebelling against them.

Perhaps the most distressing of all methods of underhanded manipulation the Party employs is the condemnation of all emotional bonds between people. Children are taught from a very young age to betray their parents at the slightest hint of unorthodoxy, causing the family unit to separate. People are isolated from each other, making them feel helpless and preventing any joint action against the Party.

Like Winston's family, relations are split by battles over food and shelter, these having been taken away by the Party to further this occurrence. People are forbidden to marry for love, and even sex in marriage is forbidden unless absolutely no pleasure is derived from it. Sex, also called "the duty to the Party," serves one purpose only: to beget children, fresh minds ripe for the brainwashing. The love between Julia and Winston, Winston believes, would be the downfall of the Party, their love an open act of political rebellion, "a blow struck against the Party." Winston's eventual betrayal of Julia under torture is what breaks his mind in the end; the Party has won once Winston abolishes his love for Julia, and in doing so, his humanity, giving in to finally loving Big Brother.

The themes of the novel 1984 are many, as the satirical parable serves a moralistic role in warning all readers of what the future might and could look like. The theme of language control is highly emphasized, almost to a philosophical standpoint, whether the language limits thought or thought limits the language. Appearance versus reality, also referred to as doublethink, shows the frailty of the human mind, when logic can fail and fold to the current of insanity, which pulls one willingly with the flow. The destruction of human values theme warns that as people become less interested in their values and morals as human beings, they will fall prey to the fascist regimes which would take advantage of such degeneration. The danger of permanent totalitarianism, perhaps Orwell's most heavily emphasized message, is demonstrated in every aspect of the novel. If every other idea were to be missed by the average reader, he would not miss the obvious squalor and hopeless existence in the world of 1984. In the end, the Party wins, humanity loses, and freedom is forever lost to the tyrannical machine known as Ingsoc.

# Quiz 1

1. **Winston is afraid of**
   A. dogs
   B. rats
   C. slugs
   D. worms

2. **Julia is a member of the**
   A. Junior Anti-Sex League
   B. Inner Party
   C. Spies
   D. Brotherhood

3. **"Facecrime" is**
   A. defacing a poster of Big Brother
   B. wearing an improper expression on your face
   C. any act which appears on the surface to be illegal, but is not
   D. spraying graffiti on the outside of a building

4. **Winston's hostile and glaring colleague in the Records Department is named**
   A. Ogilvy
   B. Tillotson
   C. Syme
   D. Ampleforth

5. **The sash around Julia's waist is**
   A. scarlet
   B. gold
   C. green
   D. white

6. **Complete the slogan: "Who controls the past, controls the future; . . ."**
   A. "...who controls the past also controls the present."
   B. "...who controls the present, controls the past."
   C. "...who controls the present also controls the future."
   D. "...who controls the future, controls the present."

7. **Comrade Ogilvy is**
   A. a war hero-turned-traitor who evaded capture and disappeared
   B. a fictitious person created by Winston for a rewritten Times article
   C. a fellow worker of Julia's in the Fiction Department
   D. Winston's neighbor in the Records Department

8. **Both Syme and Parsons ask Winston if he has any spare**
   A. Victory cigarettes
   B. shaving cream
   C. chocolate
   D. razor blades

9. **Winston predicts that all of the following will be vaporized except:**
   A. Parsons
   B. himself
   C. Syme
   D. O'Brien

10. **All of the following are (presumably) vaporized except:**
    A. Parsons
    B. Winston
    C. Syme
    D. O'Brien

11. **At the climax of the Two Minutes Hate, Goldstein's face turns into the face of**
    A. a sheep
    B. a Eurasian
    C. Big Brother
    D. a rat

12. **Winston reflects that the only thing "cheap and plentiful" is**
    A. synthetic gin
    B. Victory coffee
    C. tea
    D. sugar

13. **Complete the slogan: War is Peace; Freedom is Slavery; Ignorance is**
   A. Strength
   B. Knowledge
   C. Bliss
   D. Truth

14. **According to Syme, what is "orthodoxy"?**
   A. a type of religion which was to be outlawed
   B. strict adherence to the ideas in and language of old English literature
   C. unconsciousness
   D. fanaticism

15. **According to Winston, where does hope lie?**
   A. with the Brotherhood
   B. with the proles
   C. with Emmanuel Goldstein
   D. with O'Brien

16. **The current name of Britain is**
   A. Ingsoc
   B. Oceania
   C. Province U-571
   D. Airstrip One

17. **What is the nickname the proles have for rocket bombs?**
   A. bangers
   B. boomers
   C. steamers
   D. whoppers

18. **In his diary, Winston defines freedom as**
   A. a state where telescreens and the Thought Police do not exist
   B. the freedom to say that two plus two make four
   C. something he once dreamed about
   D. the promise of the future

19. **Winston identifies the voice that says "We shall meet in the place where there is no darkness" as belonging to whom?**

A. Winston's mother
B. Big Brother
C. Julia
D. O'Brien

20. **What did Winston steal from his younger sister?**

A. her favorite toy
B. chocolate
C. milk
D. soup

21. **Mr. Charrington offers to sell Winston a print of:**

A. St. Clement's Dane
B. Old Bailey
C. St. Martin's
D. Shoreditch

22. **Inside the glass paperweight is a**

A. seashell
B. rose
C. sea anemone
D. piece of pink coral

23. **Why do tears spring to Rutherford's eyes in the Chestnut Street Cafe?**

A. A song, "Under the spreading chestnut tree, I sold you and you sold me," is played over the telescreen
B. He is overjoyed at the news that Oceania has won a major battle over Eastasia
C. The Victory Gin is too strong for him
D. Jones and Aaronson are reminiscing about the past

24. **The caption on the Big Brother posters says:**

A. Big Brother is watching you
B. Big Brother loves you
C. Big Brother will save you
D. Big Brother knows where you live

25. **After a dream of seeing the girl in the Golden Country, Winston awakens with a word on his lips. What is the word?**
   A. "Mother"
   B. "Milton"
   C. "Julia"
   D. "Shakespeare"

# Quiz 1 Answer Key

1. **(B)** rats
2. **(A)** Junior Anti-Sex League
3. **(B)** wearing an improper expression on your face
4. **(B)** Tillotson
5. **(A)** scarlet
6. **(B)** "...who controls the present, controls the past."
7. **(B)** a fictitious person created by Winston for a rewritten Times article
8. **(D)** razor blades
9. **(A)** Parsons
10. **(D)** O'Brien
11. **(A)** a sheep
12. **(A)** synthetic gin
13. **(A)** Strength
14. **(C)** unconsciousness
15. **(B)** with the proles
16. **(D)** Airstrip One
17. **(C)** steamers
18. **(B)** the freedom to say that two plus two make four
19. **(D)** O'Brien
20. **(B)** chocolate
21. **(A)** St. Clement's Dane
22. **(D)** piece of pink coral
23. **(A)** A song, "Under the spreading chestnut tree, I sold you and you sold me," is played over the telescreen
24. **(A)** Big Brother is watching you
25. **(D)** "Shakespeare"

# Quiz 2

1. **Which line of the nursery rhyme does Julia add to what Winston already knows?**
   A. "'When I grow rich,' say the bells of Shoreditch"
   B. "'When will you pay me?' say the bells of Old Bailey"
   C. "'You owe me three farthings,' say the bells of St. Martin's"
   D. "'Oranges and lemons,' say the bells of St. Clement's"

2. **What thought does Winston have regarding chess at the end of the book?**
   A. the white knight is the piece that will invariably mate
   B. white always mates; black has never won
   C. white and black win the same number of games in the end
   D. black always mates; white has never won

3. **Why, according to O'Brien, are people brought to the Ministry of Love?**
   A. to make them confess
   B. to punish them
   C. to cure them
   D. to behave as guinea-pigs for new torture instruments

4. **According to the Party, what two groups are free?**
   A. Inner Party members and slaves
   B. proles and Inner Party members
   C. slaves and proles
   D. proles and animals

5. **What does O'Brien use as a pretext for giving Winston his address?**
   A. an invitation to a party at his flat
   B. an invitation to look at his copy of the Eleventh Edition of the Newspeak Dictionary
   C. an invitation to look at his copy of the Ninth Edition of the Newspeak Dictionary
   D. an invitation to look at his copy of the Tenth Edition of the Newspeak Dictionary

6. **What is Julia's work at the Ministry of Truth?**
   A. running and servicing the novel-writing machines in the Fiction Department
   B. sifting through articles to find references to unpersons
   C. correcting "errors and misprints" in the Records Department
   D. helping to compile the Eleventh Edition of the Newspeak Dictionary

7. **Winston finds that what he had hoped was a riot was in fact**
   A. a brawl in a pub
   B. a pro-Party rally
   C. mass disappointment at a shortage of tin saucepans
   D. an organized demonstration against Eurasia

8. **Which of the following is NOT an effect of war becoming continuous?**
   A. it heightens efficiency and accuracy in measurements and documentation of facts
   B. it ceases to be dangerous
   C. it preserves the mental atmosphere required by a hierarchical society
   D. peace

9. **According to "the book," which country will win the international war?**
   A. Oceania
   B. Eurasia
   C. Eastasia
   D. None of the above

10. **The ultimate goal of the Party is**
   A. wealth
   B. social equality
   C. peace
   D. power

11. **What, says O'Brien, is in Room 101?**
   A. the worst thing in the world, which is different for each individual
   B. an interrogation committee
   C. rats
   D. an execution squad

12. **What is Winston's "final victory over himself"?**
   A. his betrayal of Julia
   B. his final rejection of his memories
   C. the burning of his diary
   D. his ability to love Big Brother at last

13. **Winston's medical malady is a**
   A. bad back
   B. varicose ulcer
   C. club foot
   D. weak ankle

14. **Winston works in the**
   A. Ministry of Love
   B. Ministry of Peace
   C. Ministry of Truth
   D. local cigarette factory

15. **Every day, all Party members must participate in the**
   A. Truth Telling
   B. Love and Peace Exercise
   C. Two Minutes Hate
   D. Big Brother Rally

16. **In the novel, Oceania is at war with**
   A. Eurasia and Eastasia
   B. China and Africa
   C. Eurasia and Africa
   D. Eastasia and Africa

17. **Winston and Julia begin their physical love affair in**
   A. Winston's apartment
   B. a secluded wooded area in the country
   C. a secret room in the Ministry of Truth
   D. O'Brien's apartment

18. **The following are arrested for thoughtcrime:**
   A. Parsons
   B. Winston
   C. Ampleforth
   D. all of the above

19. **Who is revealed to be a member of the Thought Police?**
   A. Mr. Charrington
   B. Syme
   C. Ampleforth
   D. Julia

20. **What does Winston buy from Mr. Charrington's shop?**
   A. a diary
   B. an old oak desk
   C. a piece of silk ribbon
   D. a book of poetry

21. **True or false: Winston is married.**
   A. n/a
   B. n/a
   C. true
   D. false

22. **True or false: Winston has children.**
   A. n/a
   B. n/a
   C. true
   D. false

23. **Julia is a covert member of the Thought Police.**
   A. n/a
   B. n/a
   C. true
   D. false

24. **True or false: Parsons' daughter reports him as a criminal.**
   A. n/a
   B. n/a
   C. true
   D. false

25. **Prisoner torture takes place in the**

A. Ministry of War
B. Ministry of Hate
C. Ministry of Love
D. Ministry of Peace

# Quiz 2 Answer Key

1. **(B)** "'When will you pay me?' say the bells of Old Bailey"
2. **(B)** white always mates; black has never won
3. **(C)** to cure them
4. **(D)** proles and animals
5. **(D)** an invitation to look at his copy of the Tenth Edition of the Newspeak Dictionary
6. **(A)** running and servicing the novel-writing machines in the Fiction Department
7. **(C)** mass disappointment at a shortage of tin saucepans
8. **(A)** it heightens efficiency and accuracy in measurements and documentation of facts
9. **(D)** None of the above
10. **(D)** power
11. **(A)** the worst thing in the world, which is different for each individual
12. **(D)** his ability to love Big Brother at last
13. **(B)** varicose ulcer
14. **(C)** Ministry of Truth
15. **(C)** Two Minutes Hate
16. **(A)** Eurasia and Eastasia
17. **(B)** a secluded wooded area in the country
18. **(D)** all of the above
19. **(A)** Mr. Charrington
20. **(A)** a diary
21. **(C)** true
22. **(D)** false
23. **(D)** false
24. **(C)** true
25. **(C)** Ministry of Love

# Quiz 3

1. **The official language of Oceania is**
   A. English
   B. Ingspeak
   C. Newspeak
   D. New English

2. **What favor does Winston do for Mrs. Parsons?**
   A. traps a mouse
   B. patches her wall
   C. unclogs her sink
   D. cleans her kitchen floor

3. **What does the old man in the pub ask the bartender for?**
   A. a lager
   B. a liter
   C. a pitcher
   D. a pint

4. **Winston's last name is**
   A. Ampleforth
   B. Alder
   C. Jones
   D. Smith

5. **Julia's last name is**
   A. unknown
   B. Ampleforth
   C. Adler
   D. Smith

6. **Who tortures Winston?**
   A. Winston
   B. Syme
   C. Jones
   D. O'Brien

7. **What does Winston call the beautiful place he sees in his dreams?**
   A. The Clear Field
   B. Paradise
   C. The Golden Country
   D. Heaven

8. **What hangs in Mr. Charrington's rented room?**
   A. a full length mirror
   B. a swing
   C. the walls are bare
   D. a twelve hour clock

9. **Julia works in the**
   A. Ministry of Hate
   B. Ministry of Love
   C. Ministry of Peace
   D. Ministry of Truth

10. **Julia had her first affair at age**
   A. 16
   B. 21
   C. 25
   D. 30

11. **The Party claims to have invented the**
   A. written word
   B. airplane
   C. English language
   D. cigarette

12. **Winston often dreams of his**
   A. mother
   B. brother
   C. wife
   D. death

13. **True or false: Winston lived before the Revolution.**
   A. n/a
   B. n/a
   C. true
   D. false

14. **True or false: Julia lived before the Revolution.**
   A. n/a
   B. n/a
   C. true
   D. false

15. **The non-Party members are termed**
   A. proles
   B. citizens
   C. non-P's
   D. norms

16. **True or false: Julia is married.**
   A. n/a
   B. n/a
   C. true
   D. false

17. **True or false: Julia once worked in Pornosec.**
   A. n/a
   B. n/a
   C. true
   D. false

18. **Where are Winston and Julia arrested?**
   A. in the Golden Country
   B. in Winston's apartment
   C. at the Ministry of Truth
   D. in Mr. Charrington's rented room

19. **Who reports Winston and Julia?**
   A. Mr. Charrington
   B. Parsons
   C. Syme
   D. Ampleforth

20. **What is the name of the cafe Winston frequents?**
   A. Apple Tree Cafe
   B. Chestnut Tree Cafe
   C. Cafe Oceania
   D. Victory Cafe

21. **One Party children's organization is the**
   A. Honesty League
   B. Spies and Youth League
   C. Truth League
   D. Little Brotherhood

22. **A tool Winston often uses at work is the**
   A. physicalwrite
   B. speakwrite
   C. vocalwrite
   D. thinkwrite

23. **The Party uniform is**
   A. blue overalls
   B. black overalls
   C. white overalls
   D. orange overalls

24. **The Inner Party uniform is**
   A. blue overalls
   B. black overalls
   C. green overalls
   D. white overalls

25. **Who insists "We are the dead"?**

A. Mr. Charrington

B. Parsons

C. Winston

D. Julia

# Quiz 3 Answer Key

1. **(C)** Newspeak
2. **(C)** unclogs her sink
3. **(D)** a pint
4. **(D)** Smith
5. **(A)** unknown
6. **(D)** O'Brien
7. **(C)** The Golden Country
8. **(D)** a twelve hour clock
9. **(D)** Ministry of Truth
10. **(A)** 16
11. **(B)** airplane
12. **(A)** mother
13. **(C)** true
14. **(D)** false
15. **(A)** proles
16. **(D)** false
17. **(C)** true
18. **(D)** in Mr. Charrington's rented room
19. **(A)** Mr. Charrington
20. **(B)** Chestnut Tree Cafe
21. **(B)** Spies and Youth League
22. **(B)** speakwrite
23. **(A)** blue overalls
24. **(B)** black overalls
25. **(C)** Winston

# Quiz 4

1. **What sings to Winston and Julia at their first meeting?**
   A. a robin
   B. a mockingbird
   C. a thrush
   D. a blackbird

2. **The Party's required morning exercise routine is called**
   A. the Physical Ten
   B. the Mini Exercise
   C. the Ten Minutes Exercise
   D. the Physical Jerks

3. **Julia has to delay a rendevous with Winston because**
   A. she has a project to finish at work
   B. she has her menstrual cycle
   C. she is injured at a rally
   D. she has to meet with O'Brien

4. **True or false: Julia puts on make up and scent to please Winston.**
   A. n/a
   B. n/a
   C. true
   D. false

5. **True or false: Julia and Winston discuss double suicide.**
   A. n/a
   B. n/a
   C. true
   D. false

6. **True or false: Julia and Winston believe they are part of an underground conspiracy against the Party.**
   A. n/a
   B. n/a
   C. true
   D. false

7. **True or false: Julia and Winston are part of an underground conspiracy against the party.**
   A. n/a
   B. n/a
   C. true
   D. false

8. **After being released, Winston and Julia**
   A. do not reunite, despite running into each other
   B. find each other and live together happily
   C. commit double suicide
   D. never see each other again

9. **Winston lives**
   A. with Julia
   B. in a commune
   C. alone
   D. with his wife and children

10. **Who initiates Winston and Julia's relationship?**
   A. Winston
   B. Syme
   C. Julia
   D. O'Brien

11. **Goldstein's supposed book is entitled:**
   A. "History of Our Party"
   B. "Theory and Practice of Ingsoc"
   C. "Theory and Practice of Oligarchical Collectivism"
   D. "Oceania, Past and Present"

12. **The world contains how many nations?**
   A. 2
   B. 3
   C. 5
   D. 7

13. **What city do Winston and Julia live in?**
   A. London
   B. Chicago
   C. New York
   D. Paris

14. **Oceania's national anthem is**
   A. Oceania, our Home
   B. Big Brother is Our Savior
   C. Oceania 'tis of thee
   D. Thanks to the Party

15. **While his mind wanders, Winston writes this in his diary.**
   A. two plus two is four
   B. down with big brother
   C. death to Oceania
   D. love to big brother

16. **What Newspeak word does Winston use to describe Katharine?**
   A. goodthinkful
   B. superplusgood
   C. pluscold
   D. badthinkful

17. **What does Parsons' daughter claim he said in his sleep?**
   A. down with Big Brother
   B. Goldstein is God
   C. Newspeak is dead
   D. down with Oceania

18. **What does Katharine describe as her "duty to the Party"?**
   A. participating in the Two Minutes Hate
   B. volunteering at the Ministry of Truth
   C. participating in Hate Week
   D. having sex with Winston for purposes of procreation

19. **Who reads "the book"?**
A. Parsons
B. Winston
C. Syme
D. Julia

20. **What does the hidden telescreen first say to Winston and Julia?**
A. you have been caught
B. you are the dead
C. you are trapped
D. don't move

21. **At the end of the novel, Winston realizes**
A. he hates Julia
B. he hates Oceania
C. he loves Goldstein
D. he loves Big Brother

22. **How many women does Winston reveal having slept with?**
A. 1
B. 2
C. 3
D. 4

23. **What age group does Winston fall into?**
A. 20s-30s
B. 30s-40s
C. 40s-50s
D. 50s-60s

24. **How does Winston receive assignments at work?**
A. via e-mail
B. verbally
C. in sealed envelopes sent through interoffice mail
D. through a tube dispenser

25. **What do Winston and Julia drink with O'Brien?**
   A. scotch
   B. beer
   C. wine
   D. real coffee

# Quiz 4 Answer Key

1. **(C)** a thrush
2. **(D)** the Physical Jerks
3. **(B)** she has her menstrual cycle
4. **(C)** true
5. **(C)** true
6. **(C)** true
7. **(D)** false
8. **(A)** do not reunite, despite running into each other
9. **(C)** alone
10. **(C)** Julia
11. **(C)** "Theory and Practice of Oligarchical Collectivism"
12. **(B)** 3
13. **(A)** London
14. **(C)** Oceania 'tis of thee
15. **(B)** down with big brother
16. **(A)** goodthinkful
17. **(A)** down with Big Brother
18. **(D)** having sex with Winston for purposes of procreation
19. **(B)** Winston
20. **(B)** you are the dead
21. **(D)** he loves Big Brother
22. **(C)** 3
23. **(B)** 30s-40s
24. **(D)** through a tube dispenser
25. **(C)** wine

# ClassicNotes

# GradeSaver™

*Getting you the grade since 1999™*

## Other ClassicNotes from GradeSaver™

1984
Absalom, Absalom
Adam Bede
The Adventures of Augie March
The Adventures of Huckleberry Finn
The Adventures of Tom Sawyer
The Aeneid
Agamemnon
The Age of Innocence
Alice in Wonderland
All My Sons
All Quiet on the Western Front
All the King's Men
All the Pretty Horses
The Ambassadors
American Beauty
Angela's Ashes
Animal Farm
Anna Karenina
Antigone
Antony and Cleopatra
Aristotle's Ethics
Aristotle's Poetics
Aristotle's Politics
As I Lay Dying
As You Like It
Astrophil and Stella
The Awakening
Babbitt
The Bacchae
Bartleby the Scrivener
The Bean Trees
The Bell Jar
Beloved
Benito Cereno
Beowulf
Bhagavad-Gita
Billy Budd
Black Boy
Bleak House
The Bloody Chamber
Bluest Eye
The Bonfire of the Vanities
Brave New World
Breakfast at Tiffany's
The Brothers Karamazov
Call of the Wild
Candide
The Canterbury Tales
Cat's Cradle
Catch-22
The Catcher in the Rye
The Caucasian Chalk Circle
The Cherry Orchard
The Chosen
A Christmas Carol
Chronicle of a Death Foretold
Civil Disobedience
Civilization and Its Discontents
A Clockwork Orange
The Color of Water
The Color Purple
Comedy of Errors
Communist Manifesto
A Confederacy of Dunces
Confessions
Connecticut Yankee in King Arthur's Court
The Consolation of Philosophy
Coriolanus
The Count of Monte Cristo
Crime and Punishment
The Crucible
Cry, the Beloved Country
The Crying of Lot 49
Cymbeline
Daisy Miller
Death in Venice
Death of a Salesman
The Death of Ivan Ilych
Democracy in America
Devil in a Blue Dress
Dharma Bums
The Diary of Anne Frank
Disgrace
Divine Comedy-I: Inferno
A Doll's House
Don Quixote Book I
Don Quixote Book II
Dr. Faustus
Dr. Jekyll and Mr. Hyde
Dracula
Dubliners
East of Eden
Emma

For our full list of over 250 Study Guides, Quizzes, Sample College Application Essays, Literature Essays and E-texts, visit:

**www.gradesaver.com**

Printed in Great Britain
by Amazon

51086088R00068